Managerial Control and Performance

Managerial Control and Performance

William A. McEachern
University of Connecticut

Lexington Books
D.C. Heath and Company
Lexington, Massachusetts
Toronto   London

Grateful acknowledgment is made for use of material reprinted herein: Quotes by R. Joseph Monsen, Jr. and Anthony Downs on pp. 46, 104, and 105, © 1965 by *The Journal of Political Economy*, University of Chicago, reprinted with permission; Quotes by Robin Marris on pp. 37 and 65, copyright © 1969 by National Affairs, Inc., reprinted with permission.

Library of Congress Cataloging in Publication Data

McEachern, William A
  Managerial control and performance.

  Bibliography: p.125
  Includes index.
  1. Incentives in industry. 2. Executives, Rating of. 3. Compensation management. I. Title.
HF5549.5.I5M19   658.31'42   75-21736
ISBN 0-669-00160-0

Copyright © 1975 by D.C. Heath and Company

All rights reserved. No part of this publication may be reproduced or transmitted in any form or by any means, electronic or mechanical, including photocopy, recording, or any information storage or retrieval system, without permission in writing from the publisher.

Published simultaneously in Canada

Printed in the United States of America

International Standard Book Number: 0-669-00160-0

Library of Congress Catalog Card Number: 75-21299

To Pat

Contents

	List of Figures and Tables	ix
	Preface	xi
Chapter 1	**Introduction**	1
	Dissatisfaction with Profit as Goal of the Firm	2
	Empirical Research	3
	An Alternative Approach	5
	Organization of Study	6
Chapter 2	**A Review of the Alternative Theories of the Firm**	7
	A Review of the Alternative Theories	7
	A Summary and Comparison of Alternative Models	16
Chapter 3	**A Review of the Empirical Work**	21
	Introduction	21
	Financial Incentives of Managers	22
	Constraints on Managerial Discretion	32
	The Effects of the Separation of Ownership from Control	38
	Summary of the Empirical Work	54
Chapter 4	**Management Incentives and Constraints Under Three Different Control Conditions**	57
	Introduction	57
	Incentives and Constraints Based on Control Type	58
	Statistical Test of the Impact of Control Type on Compensation Structure	67
	Job Tenure Based on Control	84
	Summary and Conclusions	86
Chapter 5	**Management Performance Under Three Control Conditions**	89
	Introduction	89
	Stockholder Welfare Based on Three Control Conditions	89

	Retention Policy Based on Control Type	93
	Risk and Control Type	101
	Summary	107
Chapter 6	**Summary and Concluding Remarks**	109
	The Alternative Theories	109
	Previous Empirical Work	110
	An Alternative Approach	112
	Conclusions	114
	Appendixes	115
	A Owner-Manager's Incentive Structure	117
	B Calculation of Executive Compensation	119
	C The Sample	123
	Bibliography	125
	Index	135
	About the Author	139

List of Figure and Tables

Figure

4-1	Manager's Income-Staff Trade-Off	63

Tables

2-1	Output Rate Responses to Displacements from Equilibrium	16
4-1	Definitions of Control	61
4-2	Predicted Signs of the Four Sets of Hypotheses	78
4-3	Significance Levels Based on T and F Tests	81
4-4	Comparison of OM and MC Firms	83
C-1	Industry Sample	123
C-2	Large Sample	124

Preface

Although economists since the days of Adam Smith have been concerned with what has come to be known as the separation of ownership from control in the large corporation, the explicit formulation of alternative theories of the firm has appeared only within the past twenty years. More recently empirical researchers have attempted to test some implications of the alternative theories by examining the manager's incentives and constraints as well as testing for differences in performance based on the form of stockholder control prevailing in the firm. Nearly all studies of the latter type have sorted firms into those firms with a dominant stockholding interest and those without a dominant interest. If no difference was observed between the two groups, then this was viewed as evidence that the manager, even in the absence of dominant stockholder influence, was motivated by other forces to behave in the stockholders' interest.

The results of this empirical work have often appeared confusing and contradictory, and have thus far shed little light on the theory of the firm. Some of this confusion, particularly with reference to the profitability studies, can be traced to the statistical procedures employed, and to faulty or misleading interpretations of results. But the primary shortcoming of previous examinations of firm performance based on the type of control is that all studies sorted firms into only two categories, when the theoretical arguments presented by the alternative theories imply behavior associated with three distinct groups.

The empirical work coupled under the heading of "owner-controlled" those firms in which the chief executive was also the dominant stockholder with those firms in which the chief executive was under the direction of a dominant stockholder outside the firm. If firms are to be sorted at all based on control categories, a sorting procedure which permits one to focus on the chief executive's incentives and constraints in each firm involves a threefold classification of firms including: (1) owner-managed firms, (2) externally-controlled firms, which have a hired manager but an outside dominant stockholding interest, and (3) manager-controlled firms, which are firms with no dominant stockholding interest.

After examining the managers' and stockholders' incentive structure under each of the three control conditions several hypotheses are developed and tested concerning differences in management incentives and firm performance based on control. Both the theoretical formulation and empirical results indicate that the threefold classification of control proves to be a more fertile and less ambiguous procedure for categorizing firms than the previously used twofold classification system.

The idea for this study evolved from a brief paper concerning the "free-rider" problem and corporate control. I would like to thank James Buchanan for his comments on that paper and for encouraging me to develop the points in it. I would also like to thank William Beazer who read an earlier version of this study and made helpful suggestions. Most of all I owe a special debt to Roger Sherman who provided advice and encouragement at every stage of the development. He suggested a number of important revisions and helped clarify my thinking on many points. Responsibility for remaining shortcomings, of course, remains with me.

My father, Archie, and late mother, Ann, also deserve special recognition for they fostered in me the curiosity to learn, and they continually encouraged my academic efforts. Finally, I owe a deep-felt thanks to my wife, Pat, who provided not only continued support and encouragement, but served as typist and managing editor through several revisions of this study. And she did all this with skill, care, and good humor.

This research was supported in part by the National Science Foundation through Grant GS31400X. Computer support was also provided by the computer centers at the University of Virginia and the University of Connecticut.

Managerial Control and Performance

1 Introduction

Economists have long expressed dissatisfaction with the neoclassical assumption concerning the hired manager's single-minded pursuit of profits, particularly in those situations where the manager is insulated from both product market and stockholder constraints. About 200 years ago Adam Smith discussed the consequences for efficiency of the separation of ownership from control. His remarks about the joint stock company captured much of the current concern about managerial behavior: "The directors of such companies, however [are] the managers rather of other people's money than their own. . . . Negligence and profusion, therefore, must always prevail, more or less, in the management of the affairs of such a company [122, p. 700]." Alfred Marshall later observed a similar tendency for the management in the typical joint stock company to subordinate the profit objectives as a result of "negligence" [85, pp. 317-18]. John Maynard Keynes also claimed that "profits become quite secondary" when the manager's behavior goes unchecked by an ownership interest [62, p. 316]. The separation of ownership from control in the modern corporation became an issue in the 1930s with the publication of the study by Adolf Berle and Gardiner Means, entitled *The Modern Corporation and Private Property*. This study concluded that, because of the growing dispersion of stock ownership, control of the large corporation was passing from the stockholders to the managers [15]. And in the firm where the manager was in control, Berle and Means questioned the assumption that the manager would "choose to operate it in the interests of the owners" [15, p. 113].

Beginning in the latter part of the 1930s alternative goals began to emerge which could replace profit maximization. A brief introduction to these alternative goals along with a discussion of other dissatisfaction voiced concerning the goal of profit maximization will be presented in the first section. The empirical work bearing on the alternative goals of management will be introduced next. In the third section some shortcomings of this empirical work will be discussed and an alternative way of viewing the issue of the separation of ownership from control will be examined. In the final section the organization of this study will be outlined. Note that this chapter is intended to serve only as a brief introduction to topics that will be discussed in greater detail in subsequent chapters.

Dissatisfaction with Profit as Goal of the Firm

In the latter part of the 1930s alternative goals to that of profit maximization began to appear in the literature. Norman S. Buchanan argued that managers had a strong incentive to increase firm size because of the increase in salary and "psychic" income resulting "from controlling a large enterprise *per se*" [20, p. 82].

Robert A. Gordon published a comprehensive study in the 1940s dealing with executive motivation in the large corporation. He concluded that the managers are interested in the "power" that goes with the large corporation: "Power thus secured increases with the size of the firm. Here lies an important explanation of the tendency of many firms to become larger, even if sometimes the profitability of such expansion is open to serious question [48, pp. 305-306]." Gordon argued that the size of the firm also satisfies the goal of security: "The desire for security appears to have increased [among modern business leaders] . . . the large corporation caters effectively to the desire for security [48, p. 311]."

Not all the early dissatisfaction with the theory of the firm was linked to the separation of ownership from control. Some critics questioned whether profit maximization was a reasonable assumption even with an owner-manager. Benjamin Higgins pointed out that although profit maximization is a survival condition under perfect competition, its force is much weaker under "non-perfect competition" since under such conditions the entrepreneur may have the power to satisfy goals other than the goal of profits [53, p. 477]. He classified the other-than-profit entrepreneurial drives into three categories: (1) those which lead the entrepreneur to produce at a level of output below the profit maximizing output (e.g., the desire for leisure), (2) those which lead to a greater than profit maximizing output (e.g., the desire for the power and prestige associated with size), and (3) those that make him stay where he is (the force of custom or habit, and the unwillingness to take risks). Higgins was the first to use indifference-curve analysis to discuss the trade-off between profits and output—the same analysis to be used by William Baumol over twenty years later [53, pp. 477-78].

Tibor Scitovski, in challenging the traditional assumption of profit maximization, dealt more specifically with the entrepreneur's labor-leisure trade-off [114]. He concluded that the entrepreneur will maximize profits only if his choice between more income and more leisure is independent of his level of income. This would hold only if his indifference curves between income and leisure were vertical displacements of one another [114, p. 356]. In all other cases utility maximization leads to a level of output that will not maximize profits. Scitovski suggested that for this condition to hold "the combination of frugality and industry" must be "calculated to insure the independence of the entrepreneur's willingness to work from the level of income" [114, pp. 357-58]. He notes that this attitude had prevailed in the early days of capitalism and may be approximately true today.

The introduction of uncertainty may also complicate a model of profit maximization. Herbert Simon has argued that classical theory viewed man as essentially economic rather than social, and he claimed that economic man is a maximizing organism while social man is an adaptive organism [120]. Faced with a complex and uncertain economic environment, the manager may not choose to maximize profits. Instead, he may attempt to attain a certain level of profits, a certain share of the market, and a certain level of sales [120, p. 255]. Rather than maximize, the manager chooses to "satisfice," to settle for a solution which is acceptable in terms of various criteria such as survival, prestige, and aspirations, rather than a maximum of a scalar function. Simon emphasized the dynamic search process in attaining certain levels of aspiration, rather than the attainment of a long-run equilibrium. The notion of "organizational slack" developed by R.M. Cyert and J.G. March, is related to satisficing [29]. Cyert and March suggested that the quality of decision-making and the general efficiency of most organizations are often well below their full potential. The difference between actual and potential efficiency they labeled "organizational slack," which will be narrowed only in response to some pressing stimulus such as a particularly poor profit performance.

Over the past two decades several alternative formal theories have been posited, all suggesting that in the absence of strict product-market or stockholder constraints, managers will maximize something other than profits. The most widely discussed during the 1960s was William Baumol's hypothesis that firms maximize sales subject to a profit constraint [8; 9]. More recently the goal of growth maximization subject to a profit constraint as presented by Robin Marris [83] and John Kenneth Galbraith [44] has been viewed with growing interest. Perhaps the most elegant and comprehensive alternative model has been set forth by Oliver E. Williamson [139]. He developed a more explicit treatment of utility maximization than earlier writers. Finally, a less rigorous but more provocative alternative view has been presented by Harvey Leibenstein with his discussion of inefficiency resulting from the firm's failure to operate on the outer bounds of its production possibility surface [74; 75].

Empirical Research

The explicit formulation of alternative theories of the firm has been a relatively recent phenomenon, but the empirical work bearing upon managerial incentives and constraints stretches back to the 1920s. Indeed it was Berle and Means's early work on the extent of the separation of ownership from control which served as one of the primary assumptions of nearly all the discretionary theories. In view of their findings, Berle and Means asked if we have "any justification for assuming that those in control of the modern corporation will also choose to operate it in the interest of the owners?" [15, p. 113]. The answer, they argued, depends on " . . . the degree to which the self interest of those in control may run parallel to the interest of the ownership and, insofar as they differ, on the checks on the use of power which may be established by political, economic, and social conditions [15, pp. 113-14]." Thus, the Berle and Means formula for examining the effects of the separation of ownership from control is to examine how closely the manager's goals are aligned with those of stockholders, and where these goals differ to see what constraints the manager faces while seeking alternative goals.

Since the 1920s empirical work has focused on the manager's incentives and constraints. There has been a long line of studies viewing the structure and composition of the manager's income [5; 48; 70; 71; 72; 130] to see whether "the driving motives [are] the same for the executive as for individual proprietors of older days" [130, p. 3]. Another, more recent, approach to executive compensation has been the use of regression analysis to examine the relationship between executive compensation and business firm performance [7; 69; 73; 86; 88; 109]. In viewing constraints Berle and Means were the first to gather evidence concerning the distribution of corporate ownership [15], and were followed in this line of research by a series of similar studies [21; 23: 67; 69; 105; 115; 129; 133; 135].

Some economists have argued that even with the passing of a dominant interest the "economics of natural selection" will guarantee that only the most efficient firms will survive [3; 12; 41, p. 22]. But even here, Sidney Winter has shown that managers need not be forced to pursue profits exclusively if their firm has a degree of market power [141]. It follows that all the discretionary theories of the firm assume not only the separation of ownership from control, but a lack of strict competition in the product market.

If the dominant stockholder and product market constraints are relaxed, what other constraints does the manager face? Berle and Means have little faith in legal instruments available to stockholders, such as the derivative suit and the proxy contest,[a] but they see the need for a steady flow of new capital. Thus, they argue that the manager must maintain a climate in which capital is forthcoming [15, p. 247]. This is similar to the constraint employed by Baumol thirty years later [8]. The firm with poor profitability prospects will reflect a lower share price, thereby making it more difficult for the firm to grow by raising additional funds in the capital market.

---
[a] The legal instruments open to stockholders will not be explicitly treated in this study. See the author's previous research [87] for a discussion of these instruments.

The capital market can play another role in disciplining various forms of inefficiency. As Alchian and Kessel point out:

Despite the absence of competition in product markets, those who can most profitably utilize monopoly powers will acquire control over them: competition in the capital markets will allocate monopoly rights to those who can use them most profitably—the absence of competition does not imply a different quality of management . . . [4, p. 160].

The manager who sacrifices profits for other objectives and thereby allows the value of the firm's shares to slip, opens his firm to a possible take-over by an outsider interested in buying shares at the depressed level and experiencing capital gains through corporate reform. This market mechanism is the primary constraint on managerial behavior in the Marris model [83]. The effectiveness of this constraint has been a much debated issue in recent years, but in the final analysis the question concerning the effectiveness of the market for corporate control is an empirical issue. Several studies have recently been published which attempt to determine the sensitivity of this market [55; 68; 121].

The first body of research attempts to examine directly some of the manager's incentives and constraints. What are the positive and negative forces that motivate the manager to behave in the stockholder's interests? A second line of empirical work has been to focus on the separation of ownership from control to see what difference the control condition makes on managerial performance. This procedure is actually an indirect test of the effectiveness of the other incentives and constraints on the manager. Nearly all studies of this type sort firms into either firms with a controlling stockholder (owner-controlled firms) or firms without a controlling stockholder (manager-controlled firms) and proceed to compare various performance characteristics based on this difference in control type. If no significant difference in performance is observed between control types, this is seen as evidence that the manager, in the absence of a controlling stockholder, is motivated by other factors to behave as if he were an owner or under the direction of a dominant stockholder. The three performance variables that have been examined are (1) a measure of efficiency, such as net income to net worth or the returns to stockholders [17; 57; 60; 61; 69; 90; 103; 108; 125], (2) a measure of risk [17; 69; 101], and (3) a measure of retained earnings [48; 125; 139].

An Alternative Approach

All the empirical studies which examine various performance characteristics sort firms into dichotomous owner-controlled or manager-controlled categories, when three categories actually are appropriate. Under the heading of owner-controlled, firms with a dominant outside stockholder and hired manager have been grouped together with firms in which the dominant stockholder is the manager. It will be shown that attempting to test hypotheses concerning managerial discretion based on the twofold classification of control has resulted in confusing and even misleading results. If the incentives and constraints facing the manager are to be examined, a more sensible way of sorting firms is through the use of a threefold classification system consisting of: (1) firms with a controlling stockholder but a hired manager, (2) firms with a controlling stockholder who also serves as manager, and (3) firms with no controlling stockholder. When the controlling stockholder is the manager he is likely to view the discretionary aspects of the managerial position differently than if the controlling stockholder is not part of management.

Several hypotheses will be developed and tested concerning the performance characteristics of firms based on the three different control types. The performance characteristics to be examined are the managerial compensation structure, executive tenure policies, a stockholder welfare variable, firm retention policies, and firm risk. The results will show that the threefold classification of control types clears up much of the confusion found in earlier research because it allows us to focus explicitly on the incentives and constraints facing the individual managers in each category.

Organization of Study

In the next chapter the alternative theories of the firm as presented by Baumol [8; 9], Marris [83], Galbraith [43; 44], Williamson [139; 140], and Leibenstein [74; 75] will be reviewed, compared, and evaluated. The bulk of the empirical work bearing on some assumptions and implications of these alternative theories will be examined in Chapter 3. Because of the abundance of research on this subject, some of it very recent, this is a long but important chapter. Using the threefold definition of control, several hypotheses concerning managerial incentives will be developed and tested in Chapter 4, followed in Chapter 5 by the development and tests of hypotheses concerning the effects of control type on the rate of return to stockholders, the firms' retention policies, and firms' risks. The final chapter will briefly summarize the findings and state the main conclusions.

2 A Review of the Alternative Theories of the Firm

The theories of Baumol, Marris, Galbraith, Williamson, and Leibenstein will be reviewed and evaluated in the first section of this chapter. A comparison of theories and a summary of the main findings will be presented in the second section. Previous empirical work bearing on these alternative theories will be discussed in the following chapter.

A Review of the Alternative Theories

W.J. Baumol

In the first edition of *Business Behavior, Value and Growth,* William J. Baumol presents a relatively naive version of his sales maximization hypothesis. His observations as a business consultant suggested to him that sales rather than profits serve as the goal of management: "[A] program which explicitly proposes any cut in sales volume, whatever the profit considerations, is likely to meet with cold reception" [8, p. 48]. The profit level must be sufficient to pay dividends and reinvest at a rate such that the combination of dividends and share appreciation "can remunerate shareholders adequately" [8, p. 51]. Baumol argues that sales can be a long-run as well as a short-run objective, and firms consequently retain a greater proportion of earnings for future sales expansion than stockholders would prefer [8, p. 52].

Using Baumol's short-run sales maximization hypothesis, O.E. Williamson derives comparative static responses to a demand shift variable and to both proportional and lump-sum profits taxes [139, p. 80]. He finds that both output and sales will increase with an increase in demand, but will decrease with the imposition of either a proportional or a lump-sum profits tax. Since the level of output already exceeds the profit-maximizing level, output must be cut back as a result of the tax to meet the profit constraint.

In the revised edition of *Business Behavior, Value and Growth* [9], which appeared in 1967, Baumol changes the nature of the profit constraint to develop a model which allows him to compare the goals of growth, profit, and short- or long-run sales. Whereas profits act as a constraint in the earlier edition, they become an instrumental variable in the revised version

[9, p. 96]. Both dividends and retained earnings are barometers of expected profitability, and are therefore important in attracting new capital. So even in the case of short-run sales maximization, profits are necessary to attract the outside finance required to invest in sales promotion and thereby to expand sales.[a] After comparing the implications of the alternative goals, Baumol concludes that maximizing the "rate of growth" of sales revenue appears to be a better approximation of the goals of many management groups than maximizing the current level of sales [9, p. 96].

Baumol also places more emphasis in the revised edition on the link between executive salaries and business firm sales. Armed with some supportive empirical results [88; 109], he contends that managers attempt to increase firm size because "executive salaries appear to be far more closely correlated with the scale of operation of the firm than with its profitability" [9, p. 46]. He also argues that managers are less inclined to risk-taking than owners: "Gambling or risk-taking comes close to a heads you win, tails I lose affair" [9, p. 102]. If a particular gamble is successful, the executive is not likely to receive a significant permanent addition to his income because his remuneration is fairly stable. In fact, brilliant accomplishments may only raise the expectations of the stockholders for future performance. And if a gamble fails, the manager may face a hostile board of directors and possibly could lose his job. Baumol concludes that the rise of the separation of ownership from control has resulted in a more conservative management [9, p. 104].

Thus from his first edition to his revised edition Baumol goes from a static sales-maximization hypothesis, which can be easily distinguished at least conceptually from static profit maximization, to a growth-in-sales-maximization hypothesis which, as will be shown in the discussion of Marris, is more difficult to distinguish from long-term profit maximization. And his revised edition is less "impressionistic," since he is able to draw on empirical studies which appeared after the publication of the first edition [88; 109, 139]. But Baumol's minimum profit constraint remains troublesome. At one point it appears to be more of a financial constraint than a take-over constraint, because the manager with a poor profit performance is supposedly more concerned with the lack of future sources of capital than with being displaced. Yet Baumol contends that the manager who allows profits to fluctuate may lose his job. Evidently stockholders will tolerate a relatively low level of profit (as long as it is above the minimum), but they are less willing to tolerate fluctuations in profit, regardless of the average level of profitability.

---

[a] There appears to be some confusion in Baumol's model on this point. Investors respond to expected profits, and a sizable rate of expansion is required to attract venture capital. But venture capital is necessary in turn to support a sizable rate of expansion.

R. Marris

Robin Marris, drawing heavily on the work of R.A. Gordon [48], Herbert Simon [119; 120], and Edith Penrose [107], develops a growth-maximizing theory of the firm [83]. His theory relies upon both a degree of monopoly power in the product market, and a lack of strict stockholder control in the capital market. In the absence of these checks, the manager pursues size and growth because of the power, salary, status, and security that come with them. And these goods come as a combination: ". . . the individual executive rarely has the opportunity to trade off between power, salary, security, etc., because these are usually offered him in rather fixed proportions" [83, p. 64]. Marris borrows from Simon's "bureconic" theory of salary structures, which suggested that salaries have a pyramid structure in which the executive must be paid more than his subordinates. Hence the larger the firm grows, the greater the number of organizational layers, and the larger the salaries of the men at the top [83, pp. 89-99]. Managers are judged for promotion by their peers on their ability to expand the number of organizational layers through growth, rather than on their ability to contribute to the firm's profitability. For empirical support Marris, like Baumol, draws upon studies which focus on the link between executive salaries and firm sales [88; 109]. So although Marris speaks of growth maximization, he examines size-related variables (specifically, sales) to support his position.

According to Marris the firm grows by plowing profits back into new investment opportunities. As growth is pursued, the marginal return of each new venture decreases. Eventually the firm begins to experience a marginal rate of return that is below the cost of capital. And as these below-market marginal rates of return become capitalized in the share price, the market value of the firm's share drops. The firm may then become an attractive target for some reform-minded capitalist to acquire a controlling interest, reform or dismiss the growth-oriented manager, and thereby cause appreciation in the formerly depressed value of the share. Hence, expansion of the firm in excess of the level required to maximize the firm's present value is constrained by the possibility of an outside corporate raid. To preclude his being displaced in this way, the manager must turn over to the stockholders enough profit to maintain the share value at a level above that which would attract an outside raider.

Marris develops a model in which the manager pursues size while keeping the share price in a "safe region" [83, p. 43]. He posits a two-valued utility function consisting of (1) growth, and (2) the firm's valuation ratio (the firm's market value divided by its net worth). Growth by the firm is the source of salary, power, prestige, and security for the manager, while the valuation ratio is an index of security against an outside raid. As the valuation ratio grows, the risk-averse manager becomes more insulated from the market for corporate control. But since Marris notes that a large firm is more difficult to take over than a small firm [83, p. 65], growth provides security against an outside raid as well. And although Marris feels that the manager "rarely has the opportunity to trade off between power, salary, security, etc." [83, p. 64] because they are offered in fixed proportions, he nevertheless develops a model in which growth and security are traded off. Moreover, the model he develops actually has size-related security traded off against valuation-ratio-related security.

Using Marris' assumptions, Robert Solow develops a model and derives comparative dynamic responses in the growth rate of the firm to changes in the cost of capital, the discount rate, an excise tax on profits, and a proportional tax on profits. He finds based on these responses that he is unable to distinguish between the neoclassical firm and the growth maximizing firms [123, pp. 335-39]. But he is able to derive discriminating comparative dynamics by substituting a proportional tax (t) on the firm's market value for the proportional tax on the firm's profits. Then the value of growth that maximizes the present value of the firm will also maximize the present value times $(1 - t)$; but the growth maximizer, who must meet a minimum valuation constraint, will be forced by the tax to cut back on his excessive growth rate to keep his market value above the permissible minimum [123, p. 339]. All this does not say that both types of firms will have the same growth rate. Solow acknowledges that "a growth-oriented firm will choose a higher rate of growth than a profit-oriented firm" [123, p. 342]. John Williamson also shows that the growth-maximizing firm will retain a larger fraction of earnings than a profit-maximizing firm [126, p. 3]. But even here Solow notes: "The existence of a stiff personal income tax with preferential treatment of capital gains—and realized capital gains at that—is bound to make it harder to distinguish between owner-oriented and growth-oriented firms" [121, p. 339].

J.K. Galbraith

The overriding goal of Galbraith's manager is survival. The best way to ensure survival in the short run is to produce some minimum level of profits to keep stockholders content. And the best way to ensure survival in the long run is for the firm to attain a size large enough so that it is insulated from the vagaries of the product and capital markets. The manager in Galbraith's model has drives very similar to those of the manager in the Marris model, for with size comes increased "salary, expense accounts, and the individual's claim to nonsalary income or privilege" [43, p. 101], as well as "employee obeisance and peer group homage" [43, p. 101]. Although Galbraith's emphasis is on growth and not size, it is size per se that conveys the pecuniary and nonpecuniary benefits which interest the manager.

Retained earnings represent "an overwhelmingly important source of capital" [44, p. 80] in Galbraith's system. The management maintains its autonomy through retained earnings, thereby avoiding outside sources of credit and the interference that would go with them. But if profits and retained earnings should fall below some specified level, this can arouse the stockholders and "promptly revive the power of the capitalist" [44, p. 81]. At this point Galbraith appears to be bordering on the Marris take-over constraint, but he steps back, arguing that the possibility of a take-over in large corporations is "negligible" [44, p. 114]. In view of Galbraith's lack of faith in the market for corporate control, it is not clear why the management should feel threatened by aroused stockholders. Is it because the disenchanted stockholder can vote the incumbents out of office? Evidently not; Galbraith puts even less faith in the proxy machinery. "Corporate size, the passage of time and the dispersion of stock ownership do not disenfranchise the stockholder. Rather, he can vote but his vote is valueless" [44, p. 80]. Like Baumol and Marris, Galbraith views corporate size as the path to higher executive salaries: "Salaries . . . are according to scale; they do not vary with profits" [44, p. 116]. Nor does the manager's equity-related income intrude as a spur to maximizing the firm's market value since; "Stockholdings by management are small and often non-existent" [44, p. 116]. And stock options are viewed more as a "tax dodge" than as a profit incentive [44, p. 116].

Galbraith's view of the large corporation is in many ways similar to the Marris view. Indeed, at one point Galbraith concedes, "I made great use of Mr. Marris' argument. . . . In large measure I followed it" [45, p. 113]. But there are some important differences. The managers in Galbraith's firm are much more sensitive to outside interference of any kind and are much more risk averse. Galbraith's manager pursues size as a means of controlling his environment, for with size, according to Galbraith, comes an ability to manipulate supply and demand. The manager is thereby able to control the vagaries of the market place and to minimize risk [44, p. 76].

Although Galbraith's model is less rigorous than the models presented by Baumol or Marris, it is more comprehensive. In the great breadth of this argument, however, explicit substance inevitably is spread a bit thin. He deals not only with the supply of firm's resources, and the demand for its product, but he spends a large amount of time on the internal organization and decision-making process within the firm, most of which has not been touched on here. Galbraith appears more to be pointing the direction for future research rather than laying down an explicit theoretical framework.

O.E. Williamson

Oliver E. Williamson assumes that when there is separation of ownership from control and a degree of monopoly power in the product market, the manager has discretion in developing the firm's strategy. The manager's preference function consequently should be expanded to include certain expense components in addition to the usual profit term [139, pp. 28-37]. In Williamson's model the manager's utility function includes (1) the size and quality of his staff as well as the salary linked to it, (2) an emoluments term ("management slack"), defined as perquisites which, if removed, would not cause the manager to seek employment elsewhere, and (3) discretionary investment expenditures, defined as the amount by which reported earnings exceeded the minimum profit constraint. The minimum profit constraint is that amount required to keep stockholders satisfied with their investment and thus ensure the survival of the existing managerial team [139, pp. 40-41]. Williamson assumes that management slack comes out of potential profits, thereby reducing reported profits. Discretionary investment expenditures reflect any remaining excess between reported profits and the minimum profit constraint. Since the slack term and discretionary investment expenditures both reduce potential profits, neither affects the output decision. But the staff term in Williamson's model includes selling and administration costs and therefore has a sales-promotion component which affects demand and consequently affects the output decision.

Williamson, like Marris, draws upon Simon to explain a managerial expense preference for staff. An expanded staff is the path to promotion and larger salary [139, p. 34]. In addition, staff can provide increased security and can satisfy professional achievement objectives. Because of the manager's positive preference for staff, it will be employed in the range where its marginal cost exceeds its marginal productivity [139, p. 41]. And because of its demand-related component, the equilibrium rate of output will exceed that implied for the standard profit-maximizing firm. Hence some staff (and all emoluments) will be employed inefficiently.

Williamson derives comparative static responses in output and staff to a demand shift parameter, a proportional profits tax, and a lump-sum tax, and he compares the output responses with those derived from the static profit-maximizing model [139, pp. 43-49]. His results indicate that an increase in demand will cause an increase in output for both the management-discretion and profit-maximizing models. While an increase in the proportional tax or lump-sum tax has no effect on output in the profit-maximizing model, output is affected by these changes in the management-discretion model. An increase in the proportional tax rate makes staff less costly in terms of foregone discretionary profits. But this change in the proportional tax has both an income and substitution effect, making it more difficult to say for sure the direction of the resulting change in output. The positive sign derived by Williamson assumes that the manager will consume more staff as a result of its lower price, thereby increasing demand and output. An increase in the lump-sum tax causes a downward shift in the trade-off curve between staff and discretionary profits; the "price" remains the same and an income effect is all that is registered. This decrease in income results in a reduced level of staff employed. The level of output falls as well because of the impact of a reduced staff on demand.

Williamson's is a certainty model and as such he does not discuss the manager's attitude towards risk as did previous researchers. And since his analysis is static there are no direct implications as to how a firm might be expected to operate over time. But there are some hints. Although salary is tied to staff in the static analysis, Williamson indicates that over time the managers are likely to pursue firm size, "Since expansion of staff and emoluments can scarcely proceed independently of the physical facilities . . ." [139, p. 36]. Thus in a dynamic sense, an increased salary is tied to expansion of firm size. Although the firm's retention policy does not directly enter Williamson's calculus, he notes that since retained earnings are a source of discretion for the manager, retained earnings are likely to be higher if the manager has more freedom in decision-making [139, p. 135]. Thus when managers are free from stockholder and product-market constraints, they are likely to exhibit a larger retention ratio.

In spite of the limitations of a static-certainty framework, Williamson's analysis goes far in developing a theory of the firm based on the manager's utility function. But in stating his position quite explicitly, his model is more easily criticized than, say, Galbraith's, whose model in many respects is difficult to pin down. For example, Williamson's analysis assumes that although the management can use resources inefficiently, the production sector of the firm operates efficiently. The management's laxness does not seep down to the shop-floor level. Williamson's empirical findings suggest however that "labor slack" may exist as well [139, p. 91]. Indeed, he later recognizes the need for introducing the possibility of labor slack [138, p. 22]. The introduction of production inefficiency to Williamson's model would appear to make more costly the manager's diversion of profit to his own purpose. And the more obvious this diversion is to the shop floor, the greater the impact on lower level efficiency.

Another shortcoming of Williamson's model is that the minimum profit constraint is given exogenously and is independent of the nature and extent of profit diversion. But it appears that the *form* of any profit diversion may affect an existing or potential stockholder's ability to determine whether managerial reform is in order. For example the diversion of one million dollars to increased salary is likely to be more easily observed and to arouse stockholders more than diverting the same amount to expanded staff or even to obtain nonpecuniary benefits such as larger offices. Yet Williamson treats additional salary and additional perquisites identically, both in the manager's utility function and his opportunity set. It appears easier to conceal profit diversion through increased emoluments than through additional salary; after all, the salary data appear in the annual proxy statements.

H. Leibenstein

Harvey Leibenstein presents the basic point that, in the absence of strict competition in the product market, firms do not produce on the outer bounds of their production possibility surface [74; 75]. His emphasis is not on profit diversion as such, but on the lack of cost minimization and the failure to adopt the most efficient technological innovations, a shortcoming he would label "X-inefficiency." Leibenstein cites particular instances where, either as a result of advice or as a consequence of a perceived "crisis," firms undertake changes that frequently result in startling increases in output per man [74, pp. 404-406]. He notes that since most employees receive no vested rights in the stream of gains resulting from a particular innovation, there is a resistance to change that may appear irrational to an observer. Nor are the managers or supervisors likely to push production to the frontier since disturbing others, upsetting interpersonal relations, and so on are apt to generate a greater personal disutility than justified by the personal gains of making the move to the more efficient point.

Leibenstein's formulation is not new. A similar point was made by J.R. Hicks in 1935 when he argued that

. . . people in monopolistic positions . . . are likely to exploit their advantages much more by not bothering to get very near the position of maximum profit, than by straining themselves to get very close to it. The best of all monopoly profits is a quiet life [52, p. 8].

Leibenstein's theory also adopts elements of Simon's satisficing model; the manager accepts some solution that is "good enough." Cyert and March's notion of organizational slack is also similar to Leibenstein's X-inefficiency. All organizations are prone to slack; this slack will be tightened only in response to some definite stimulus such as a particularly bad profit performance.

M.A. Crew, M.W. Jones-Lee, and C.K. Rowley have attempted to formalize Leibenstein's analysis and derive comparative static responses in output and policing costs to increases in a demand shift parameter, a proportional profits tax, and a lump-sum tax [27]. They assume that

X-inefficiency is related directly to the firm's potential profit level. During prosperous times there is less cost consciousness and greater inefficiency. More difficult times cause a belt-tightening process throughout the firm. Both overhead and marginal costs vary in the same direction as the potential profit level. Policing costs are introduced as an attempt to minimize inefficiencies. The optimal amount of policing is that quantity which equates the marginal cost of policing with the marginal increase in efficiency. It is assumed that policing activity is more productive during prosperous times [27, pp. 177-78].

After making some fairly restrictive assumptions about the signs of the relevant first and second partial derivatives, the authors derive comparative static responses in output and policing levels to a demand shift parameter, a proportional profits tax, and a lump-sum tax [27, pp. 180-83]. Again the output response to an increase in demand is positive and provides no basis for discriminating between the "X-theory" and the profit-maximizing theory. But both types of taxes produce a negative response in output with the X-theory, versus a zero response with profit maximization. The signs that Crew, Jones-Lee, and Rowley derive for the policing costs term for the X-theory are identical to the output responses. The authors provide no intuitive explanation for their results; these results appear to depend on the somewhat tenuous assumptions concerning the signs of the relevant partial derivations.

Although Leibenstein's theory of X-efficiency is not comparable to the other alternative theories in many respects, the comparative static responses in output derived by Crew et al. for the X-theory can be compared with those derived by O.E. Williamson for his discretionary model and for the static sales-maximizing model. The results for changes in a demand shift parameter (D), a proportional tax on profits (t), and the lump-sum tax (T) are given in table 2-1, where the alternative theories are contrasted with the profit-maximization theory. All theories predict an increased output with an increase in demand. With a proportional tax on profits the sales-maximization theory and X-theory predict a reduction in output, while Williamson's discretionary model predicts a questionable positive sign (recall that income and substitution effects could not be clearly sorted out). The three alternative theories can be distinguished from profit maximization with an increase in a lump-sum tax, but the alternative theories cannot be distinguished from one another. Solow's comparison of the comparative dynamic responses in the firms' growth rates to changes in various parameters indicates that it also is difficult to discriminate between the growth-maximizing firm and the long-run profit-maximizing firm based on these responses. He shows that discriminating comparative dynamic responses between the two types of firms can be derived only when one considers a proportional tax on the firm's market value [123, p. 339].

Table 2-1
Output Rate Responses to Displacements from Equilibrium

		D	t	T
Profit Maximization	Q	+	0	0
Sales Maximization	Q	+	−	−
Discretionary Model	Q	+	+?	−
X-Theory	Q	+	−	−

A Summary and Comparison of the Alternative Models

Although the models by Baumol, Marris, Galbraith, and Williamson employ different assumptions, terminology, and constraints, they are more similar than they at first appear. All concern the large corporation characterized by the separation of ownership from control and a downward sloping demand curve in the product market. The manager is motivated in each case by, among other things, his desire for income and security. Baumol's manager pursues size because "executive salaries appear to be far more closely correlated with the scale of operation of the firm than with its profitability" [9, p. 46]. The manager in Marris' model pursues firm size, for along with size comes "power, salary, security, etc.," [83, p. 64] in fixed proportions. Galbraith's manager is not only interested in the salary and status that goes with firm size, but size allows the manager to avoid risks by insulating the firm from the product and capital markets [44, p. 76]. In Williamson's static analysis salary is linked to the size of staff, but in a dynamic sense staff size is linked to the size of the firm. Hence in each model salary is a size-related variable which will increase with firm expansion. Growth is pursued because it will enlarge size, but the pecuniary and nonpecuniary benefits that interest the manager are linked to size, not growth itself. Williamson has the most complex model since he permits the manager to trade off among staff, emoluments, and discretionary profits. The other three models view size as conveying an entire package of pecuniary and nonpecuniary benefits.

In each of the four models the manager tends to retain a larger fraction of earnings than stockholders would find optimal. The manager in Marris' model finances firm growth primarily out of retained earnings and he increases retention until he runs up against the minimum valuation constraint. Galbraith's manager has a deathly fear of going to the capital market because of the strings attached to outside funds, and consequently relies for expansion almost entirely on retained earnings. Although Baumol does not deal explicitly with the retention policy of the firm, John Williamson has shown that either the sales-maximizing or growth-maximizing manager will push the retention ratio "beyond the point at which the value of the firm is maximized" [137, p. 16]. The manager in O.E. Williamson's model derives no satisfaction from dividends per se, but views retained earnings as a source of discretion [139, p. 135]. Hence O.E. Williamson's manager will turn over to the stockholders just the minimum level of dividends necessary to satisfy them. Thus all four theories predict the manager will retain a larger fraction of profits than stockholders would prefer.

Each theory posits some minimum performance constraint measured either in terms of profits or the firm's market value. In all cases this minimum is determined exogenously. The managers in Baumol's and Galbraith's models are more concerned with generating profits to finance additional expansion than with being removed from office as a result of a take-over. Marris' manager is more concerned with the threat of a take-over and maintains the market value of the firm high enough to ensure survival. Williamson's minimum profit constraint is just that—some amount that must be produced to satisfy stockholders before any other activity can go on. In positing such an exogenous minimum performance constraint, the alternative theories beg the question of how much discretion does the manager actually have. How does one determine the relationship between the minimum profit constraint and the firm's potential profitability? And in making this constraint independent of the form and extent of profit diversion these theories may neglect some important considerations. An endogenous profit constraint may yield implications about the form and extent of profit diversion that do not come out of the existing models.

The theory of executive compensation in the alternative models is most troublesome. To the extent that firm expansion increases the top executive's marginal productivity, one can explain why his income may be linked to firm size. But in the alternative models, executive pay appears to be linked to size, regardless of profits (provided, of course, that the exogenously determined minimum profit level is met). Baumol contends that the manager's salary is linked to size "even if size did not promote profits" [9, p. 46]. Galbraith argues, "Salaries . . . are according to scale; they do not vary with profit" [44, p. 116]. Marris views salary and size as coming "in rather fixed proportions" [83, p. 64]. And O.E. Williamson ties salary to his "staff" term even though staff is employed above the level which maximizes profits [139, p. 34]. When income other than salary is considered, including a variety of contingent and deferred forms of compensation, the formulators of the alternative theories concede some link between the executive's total income and the firm's profit or market value. For example, Baumol feels that "by far the most important reason for management's concern for the behavior of the price of company stock is the stock option" [10, p. 81]. , Marris notes that managerial ownership in the firm, "while significantly reinforcing the incentives to maintain a reasonable valuation ratio . . . is unlikely . . . to enforce profit maximization in the ordinarily understood sense" [83, p. 77]. But Williamson and Galbraith see less of a role for various incentive schemes. Williamson argues that with incentive devices such as stock options it is often difficult to impute causality, and it is therefore difficult to reward those who are responsible for a given increase in profitability. He claims that various incentive devices also are subject to "free-rider" problems [140, pp. 300-306] because an individual's compensation depends on the actions of many individuals and not just his own actions alone. Galbraith dismisses ownership incentives with the empirical claim that "stockholdings by management are small and often non-existent" [44, p. 116]. Moreover, he views stock options as "more of a tax dodge than . . . an incentive" [44, p. 116].

Statements in the alternative theories concerning the link between firm size and managerial income assume the status of empirical fact, even though the evidence in this area is far from convincing. Galbraith, for example, relies upon the now dated work of R.A. Gordon [48] to substantiate his claim that "stockholdings by management are small and often non-existent" [44, p. 116]. Gordon's research was conducted at the depths of the depression (1935), when the manager's equity-related income was understandably low. Although evidence concerning the link between executive income and performance will be examined in the following chapter, we should note here that there is an impressive body of research linking the manager's income to the firm's profitability and its market value. In one study of fifty top corporate executives, over 70 percent of this group of executives' after-tax income was tied to equity-related sources [72]. Since the alternative theories generally have denied the existence of any substantial link between the manager's income and stockholder welfare measures such as profitability and market value, the theories have ignored some facts of obvious importance.

Finally one might ask why any manager would join a firm in which, either because of competition in the product market or because of close stockholder supervision, there was little room for managerial discretion. Why join this type of firm when one could join a firm that had higher salaries, larger staff, more perquisites, and less pressure from the product or capital markets? There is the strong implication in the theories of Baumol, Marris, Galbraith, and, particularly, Williamson that managers employed in firms which permit a wider range of discretion are more able to pursue their own goals and are absolutely better off than managers in more competitive firms or firms with closer stockholder supervision. This implies that either (a) to the extent that competition exists among executives, managers in firms that provide more discretion must be more qualified than others since these managers receive a higher total income, or (b) if the managers in both types of firms are equally qualified, then there is no competition among executives for the more attractive jobs. Armen Alchian argues that competition for jobs among executives ensures that any net advantage of one job over another will be competed away; resulting in a lower money wage for the more "attractive, easy, or secure jobs" [1, pp. 345-46]. These issues will be examined in Chapter 4.

The alternative theories we have discussed were not the first to formulate the notion that managers may have a preference for size. This idea was discussed by Frank Knight [64], Joseph A. Schumpeter [113], and Robert A. Gordon [48] long before the explicit formulation of the alternative theories. But with these earlier authors, the drive for size was not restricted to the hired or professional manager. In fact, Knight and Schumpeter discussed the tendency to "build empires" primarily in the context of the owner-entrepreneur. Shumpeter recognized as the first drive of the entrepreneur, "the dream and the will to found a kingdom" [113, p. 93]. Knight emphasized "the impulse to create," an impulse for which "increased income is not the dominant motive" [64, p. 162]. Similarly, Gordon noted that the tendency "to continue to expand in the face of declining profits . . . may be no stronger [among professional managers] than among owner-managers" [48, pp. 331-32]. Even though the theory discussing the pursuit of size was targeted initially at owner-managers, there is no room in the more recent alternative theories for owner-managers since each model is cast in an environment characterized by the separation of ownership from control.

Either implicitly or explicitly the alternative theories sort firms into two categories: (1) firms with a dominant stockholder in which the single-minded pursuit of profit prevails, and (2) firms without a dominant stockholder in which alternative goals are given vent. Empirical work aimed at examining some of the implications of the alternative theories has followed this lead by classifying firms either as having a dominant stockholder (owner-controlled firms) or without a dominant stockholder (manager-controlled firms). This line of research then proceeds to check for differences in behavior between the two sets of firms. It is presumed that the owner-controlled group behaves in the stockholders' interest while the manager-controlled group behaves in the manager's interest. And yet if no difference is observed between the two control types in variables such as the firm's retention ratio this has been viewed as evidence that both types of firms behave in the stockholders' interest. But notice that the owner-controlled group includes not only managers under the thumb of an outside dominant stockholder, but also owner-managers, who may be interested in the nonpecuniary sources of utility that would interest any other manager.

Thus the owner-managers and the managers in firms without a dominant stockholder may not behave so very differently. Indeed, while one may correctly argue that owner-managers and hired managers have different opportunity sets (since the owner is likely to have a larger stake in the firm), it is quite another matter to argue that these two groups have different goals. For reasons that will be pointed out in this study, viewing the world as consisting simply of owner-controlled and manager-controlled firms has led to confusing and misleading results, for when the dominant stockholder is the manager he can view the firm differently than when he is outside the firm. Of course the alternative theories have said little about the owner-controlled group, confining analysis mainly to the manager-controlled group. But it seems that the frame of reference of the theory should be broadened to include both firms with owner-managers and firms with a dominant stockholder but hired managers, as two additional and distinct groups.

The empirical work bearing on a test of the alternative theories has attempted to examine some of the assumptions and implications of these theories. Is the manager's income related more to the scale of the firm than to firm profit or market value? Do managers in manager-controlled firms retain a larger fraction of earnings? Are these managers more risk averse, and do they divert more profits to other-than-profit goals than managers in firms with a dominant stockholder? And, finally, how effectively does the market for corporate control discipline managers? Economists have begun to examine some of these questions by gathering empirical evidence, for in the final analysis managerial behavior in the theory of the firm is an empirical issue. In the following chapter the bulk of the recent empirical work treating the manager's incentives and constraints will be examined.

3 A Review of the Empirical Work

Introduction

The explicit formulation of alternative theories of the firm has been a relatively recent phenomenon, but the empirical work bearing upon managerial incentives and constraints stretches back to the 1920s. Indeed, it was the early empirical work on separation of ownership from control which served as one of the primary assumptions for nearly all of the theories of discretionary management behavior. In 1925, F.W. Taussig and W.F. Barker began to lay the foundation for future inquiry in noting that the control of business was passing from the "individual proprietors" or "undertakers" to the corporate employee: "Incorporated industry under salaried managers is the order of the day" [130, p. 3]. In view of this development they asked: "Are the driving motives the same for the executive as for individual proprietors of older days?" [130, p. 3]. They then proceeded to examine the composition, structure, and variability of executive compensation for a large sample of firms over a ten-year period. Similar approaches have been employed in a half dozen studies since then [5; 48; 70; 71; 72; 133]. A more recent approach to executive motivation, precipitated partly by Baumol's observations concerning the link between manager's salaries and firm size [9, p. 46], has been the use of statistical analysis to examine the relationship between executive compensation and firm size and profitability [7; 24; 69; 73; 86; 88].

Adolf Berle and Gardiner Means were the first to gather evidence concerning the distribution of corporate ownership [15]. In their analysis of stock distribution they focused on how stockholders could constrain managerial activity. They asked if we have "any justification for assuming that those in control of the modern corporation will also choose to operate it in the interests of the owners?" [15, p. 113]. The answer, they felt, depended upon the manager's incentive and constraints. How closely aligned were the goals of owners and managers and where these goals did differ, what checks existed in the economy to bring them back into line? [15, p. 114]. Much of the empirical literature examining the assumptions and implications of the alternative theories of the firm has been concerned with the managers' incentives and constraints.

A second line of empirical work has focused on the separation of ownership from control to see what difference the control condition makes on managerial performance. This procedure is actually an indirect test of the effectiveness of the other incentives and constraints on the manager. Nearly all studies of this type have sorted firms into either owner-controlled or manager-controlled categories and compared the categories along various performance characteristics. If no significant difference in performance was observed between control types, this was seen as evidence that the manager, in the absence of a controlling stockholder, was motivated by other forces to behave as if he were under the direction of a dominant stockholder. The three performance variables examined are a measure of efficiency, such as net income to net worth or the returns to stockholders [17; 57; 60; 61; 69; 90; 103; 108; 125], a measure of risk [17; 69; 101], and a measure of retained earnings [58; 125; 139]. Since this approach is relatively new (only one of the studies had been published prior to 1968), and since this literature has not been brought together elsewhere, each of the studies will be discussed and evaluted in some detail in the fourth section of this chapter.

The managers' incentives will be examined in the second section. The constraints faced by the manager will be discussed in the third section. In the fourth section, the studies viewing the effect of the separation of ownership from control will be discussed. The final section will briefly summarize the findings and state the main conclusions. The organization of our review may be viewed as follows. The second and third sections concern the question: How much discretion does the manager have? The fourth section examines the question: What difference does the presence of managerial discretion make on firm performance? Of course a number of studies deal with both of these questions and our taking them up at one point rather than another will then be somewhat arbitrary.

Financial Incentives of Managers

The literature on executive compensation may be divided into two groups: the first approach was simply to look at the size and composition of executive income; the second and more recent approach has been the use of statistical analysis to examine the relationship between executive compensation and firm performance. Since executive compensation is a commonly mentioned point at which the motives of the managers are said to differ from the goals of the owners, both strains of literature attempt to determine what financial motivation managers have to act in the interest of the stockholders. The literature taking the first approach will be examined in Part a, and the statistical work will be discussed in Part b. Another aspect of managerial motivation, the incentive for promotion and tenure, will be examined in Part c.

a. Size and Composition of Managerial Income

The first major study of this century looking at executive income was published in 1925 by Taussig and Barker [130]. They attempted to see if the hired managers of the modern corporation had the same "driving motives" as the owner-operators of the past [130, p. 3]. They examined a sample of about 100 firms in each of four size groups from 1904 to 1914 and found that the average salary in the largest group was about $10,000. Less than 5 percent of these firms appeared to have any regular method of extra compensation (bonus plans). They noted that while profits displayed the "ebb and flow" of the market place, salaries fluctuated very little during the ten-year period [130, p. 22]. During periods of poor performance it was unlikely that salaries would be reduced; rather a poor performance would result in a change in personnel [130, p. 20]. Another noteworthy finding of their study was that the top executive group in the sample of large corporations collectively owned about 18 percent of their firms' common stock [130, p. 12].

The use of professional managers increased after World War I, and with this came a substantial increase in salaries. John Calhoun Baker examined the size and composition of executive incomes between 1928 and 1936 for a sample of 59 firms drawn from the Berle and Means study [5]. He found that the average annual salary was around $70,000, but some exceeded one million dollars a year [5, p. 168]. Although salaries remained relatively inflexible during the period, bonus payments, which were sometimes used, displayed large year-to-year fluctuations [5, p. 163]. A form of stock option was also used during this period. About 25 percent to 35 percent of the companies that Baker examined gave options to one or more executives at some time during the period 1928-38 [6, p. 107]. Baker also noted that larger corporations usually paid managers more than smaller companies, regardless of earnings [6, p. 239].

Robert A. Gordon examined Baker's data more closely and concluded that executive compensation during the period was large and relatively stable [48, pp. 271-84]. Although bonus plans were quite common during the 1920s, they declined drastically during the 1930s when many companies canceled their bonus plans entirely [48, p. 286]. Where bonus plans were in use, they were applied primarily to those officers below the chief executive [48, p. 293]. Gordon calculated the market value of executive holdings and the dividends for each of the 161 top executives in his sample. The median value of holdings in 1935 was about $300,000, and the median dividend was about 1 percent of this or $3,000 [48, p. 301]. After comparing the median value of dividends with the median level of salary plus bonus ($79,300), Gordon concluded that stock ownership represented a relatively minor source of income to the manager [48, p. 301]. But one should keep in mind that he examined dividends during a period of depression and he neglected capital gains altogether.

A more recent study by Wilbur Lewellen suggests that Gordon's conclusions do not hold for later years [70; 72]. Lewellen examined the total compensation of the five highest paid executives in fifty large industrial corporations for the period 1940 to 1963. After deleting extreme values, he found that the average market value of the chief executive's stockholdings in his own firm ranged from about $400,000 in the early 1940s to over one million dollars in the early 1960s [72, pp. 97-98]. Before-tax dividends went from $20,000 to $50,000 between these periods. Capital gains were much more volatile, going from the $30,000-$60,000 range in the 1940s to the $150,000-$300,000 range in the early 1960s. While the value of managers' stockholdings increased over the period, the fraction of the average firm's common stock held by its top five executives declined from about one-quarter of a percent to one-eighth of a percent [72, p. 105].

Lewellen computed the ratio of stock-related income, consisting of capital gains and dividends plus the value of stock options, to the salary-plus-bonus portion of income. For the entire sample this ratio of stock-related to salary-related income increased from about 1.0 in the early 1940s to 6.5 in the early 1960s [72, p. 89]. With extreme values deleted, the figure went from 0.8 to 2.7 [72, p. 102]. Thus, even though the fraction of the firm owned by managers had been decreasing, the relative importance of equity-related income in the manager's total income had been growing.

Lewellen revised his study to reflect the 1964-1969 experience and found the components of the pay package expanded at about the same rate even though the tax laws of 1964 made stock options less attractive. Stock options remained an important relative and increasing absolute source of income. Deferred compensation also increased in use over the period [71].

Several trends emerge from the analysis of executive income. Bonus payments as a source of income were practically non-existent in the 1904-1914 period. They increased in popularity in the 1920s and fell out of favor during the depression, but have since become popular once again with about 65 percent of all manufacturing firms offering some type of executive bonus plan in 1969 [25, p. 10]. Deferred compensation and pension plans have also increased in use. A basic question concerning the non-salary portions of compensation, such as bonus plans plus other deferred and contingent forms of compensation, is whether these serve as specific incentive devices or are simply ways to reduce the portion of a manager's compensation that would be absorbed as taxes. Gordon found that during the 1930s bonuses appeared to be in addition to salary rather than a substitute for it, but he concluded that "bonuses have failed to relate total compensation closely to the results of leadership activity" [48, p. 296]. Roberts found that the existence of a bonus and deferred compensation plans between 1948-1950 appeared to have no particular effect on the firm's profitability [109, p. 93]. The fraction of the firm held by top executives has declined steadily since the early 1900s, but the value of equity-related income in the pay package has increased in the last twenty years. This increase was due largely to legislation in 1950 conveying favorable tax treatment to stock options. Lewellen has shown that the manager's total income has now come to be related more to the firm's equity performance. In sum, it appears that the overall trend in the design of compensation plans is towards aligning the manager's interests with those of the stockholders.

b. Compensation and Performance

As noted in the previous chapter, several alternative theories of the firm suggest that managers' incomes are more closely related to the sizes of the firms for which they work than to the firms' profits [9, p. 46; 44, p. 76; 83, p. 64; 139, p. 34]. The first line of empirical work dealing with incentives was simply a look at the size and composition of executive income. A second, more recent, approach has been to examine executive compensation in relation to various performance characteristics of the firm. This is a relevant question because if, as Baumol suggests [9, p. 46] for instance, executive pay is more closely related to size than to profitability, then the compensation structure would provide little incentive for managers to maximize profits. Studies dealing with the determinants of executive compensation may be divided into three groups. The first simply uses salary plus bonus as a definition of income. The second expands the definition of income to include various other forms of compensation. The third uses the broad definition of income and also contrasts compensation schemes based on type of control.

David Roberts was the first to test systematically the link between compensation, profits, and sales [109]. Using a sample of 77 firms in six industries he related the average compensation, defined as salary plus bonus plus deferred compensation, of the executive officers in a corporation to the firm's profitability and size for the three-year period 1948-1950. He attempted to examine inter-industry differences in the level of compensation and found these to be important [109, p. 33]. Like later researchers, he was confronted by a high degree of collinearity between dollar profits and sales and consequently was unable to sort out individual effects. He attempted to avoid the collinearity problems by examining only those cases in which the sales-profit relationship was weak. He concluded from this fragmentary evidence that "compensation is more closely related to sales than to dollar profits" [109, p. 62]. J.W. McGuire, J.S.Y. Chiu, and A.O. Elbing regressed executive salary-plus-bonus payments on firm sales and firm profits also, using a sample of 45 large industrial corporations over the seven-year period 1953-1959 [88]. They employed current values, lagged values, and first differences of all variables for each year to derive partial correlation coefficients [88, p. 758]. Their findings were consistent with Roberts'; compensation and sales were significantly related in five of the seven years, but compensation and profits were unrelated [88, p. 760].

Samuel Baker later suggested that a misspecification of the functional form may have biased earlier researchers' results [7, p. 379]. For a sample of 30 industrial firms out of the largest 100, Baker utilized a semi-log functional form and ran regressions similar to those of both Roberts and McGuire, Chiu and Elbing. For each firm he used the four-year average of the variables between 1962 and 1965. He found both profits and sales had a positive effect on executive compensation which was significant at the .05 level [7, p. 382]. More recently David H. Ciscel examined the simple correlation coefficients between the chief executive's salary-plus-bonus and the firm's sales, assets, and profits, to show that collinearity makes conclusions elusive. For a sample of 210 large corporations observed for each of the years 1969, 1970, and 1971, he found no significant difference between the simple correlation coefficients obtained for executive compensation with sales or assets and with profits [24, p. 616]. Ciscel's research does little more than underscore problems of collinearity between profits and various measures of firm size.

All of these studies were hampered by the presence of multicollinearity in variables used to explain executive compensation. Moreover, in using only salary-plus-bonus as definition of executive compensation they neglected a large portion of executive income—the manager's equity-related income—a portion of income one might expect to be tied closely to the firm's financial performance. Wilbur Lewellen broadened the definition of income to include stock options, pensions, plus other deferred compensation in his painstaking empirical study of 50 large corporations [70; 72]. Lewellen and Huntsman drew upon Lewellen's original sample to examine the determinants of executive compensation using annual observations at three-year intervals between 1940 and 1963 [73]. For their dependent variable they employed both salary-plus-bonus and total-after-tax compensation [73, pp. 712-13]. The explanatory variables used were sales and profits in one regression, and sales and the market value of the firm in another regression. As with earlier studies, they found a large degree of collinearity between the two explanatory variables, but they also found that the error term was heteroscedastic, for it appeared to vary directly with the dependent variable. They dealt with both of these problems by dividing the equation through by a scale-related deflator, the assets of the firm. This adjustment procedure yielded homoscedastic error terms and also reduced the collinearity between the explanatory variables. Their weighted regression results indicated that with both measures of compensation, "reported company profits appear to have a strong and persistent influence in executive rewards whereas sales seem to have little, if any, impact" [73, p. 718]. When the firm's market value was substituted for profits, it was also positive and significant in its effect using either definition of compensation, while sales remained insignificant. These results are somewhat surprising, running completely counter to previous findings, and yet they are the same whether the simple definition of compensation or the broader total after-tax definition of compensation is used. Part of this may be explained by their ability to overcome the problem of multi-collinearity, which had been so troublesome in earlier research.

Robert T. Masson adopted both a cross-section and a time-series approach in an effort to examine the determinants of *changes* in executive compensation [86]. Using the total after-tax income of the top three-to-five executives in 39 firms from the electronics, chemical, and aerospace industries between 1947 and 1966, he regressed year-to-year changes in income on year-to-year changes in sales, earnings per share, and the rate of return on a share of the firm's stock. After failing to derive statistically significant results for individual firms [86, p. 1284] with time-series analysis, he proceeded in cross-section to compare the signs of the time-series coefficients to test whether he did any better than a random draw of positive and negative signs. He concluded that, "a significant number of firms do have stock market return as an important determinant of executive compensation" [86, p. 1285]. And, "the hypothesis can be rejected that firms pay their executives primarily for sales maximization" [86, p. 1285]. Masson went on to show that incentives do affect performance, and stock-oriented incentives are better able to benefit stockholders than strictly profit or sales incentives [86, p. 1289].

Masson's analysis is clever and generally persuasive. He first uncovered the link between changes in executive income and changes in the firm's share in the stock market. This result is not surprising in view of Lewellen's findings [72] concerning the importance of equity related income in the pay package. Masson proceeded to show that firms in which the manager's income is tied more to market performance yield higher returns to stockholders. One problem he can't avoid, however, is that managers, as insiders, may be more able to predict the success or failure of a firm and may tend to buy into firms that have greater possibilities for future success. These purchases will increase the manager's total absolute dividends and capital gains in future time periods. Consequently, it will appear that incentives result in better performance when actually anticipated success may have prompted the share purchases. Likewise, on anticipating lean years the managers in other firms can sell off shares (or simply fail to purchase shares), thereby tying their total income less to the firms' market values. This would give the appearance that poorly performing firms have compensation packages that vary less with respect to changes in market performance than those of the more successful firms.[a]

Two studies attempted to consider the effect of the control type on the manager's compensation structure [68; 139, pp. 130-34]. O.E. Williamson, using a sample of from 25 to 30 firms over three time periods, employed salary plus bonus as the dependent variable with general administrative and selling expense, the concentration ratio of the firm's industry, a barrier-to-entry measure, plus an index for management control, all as explanatory variables [139, pp. 130-34]. Since he lacked information concerning stock distribution he used the proportion of managers on the board of directors as a measure of management control. After carrying out cross-section regressions for each period he found the salary-plus-bonus in "manager-controlled" firms significantly higher in one of the three time periods, and he viewed this evidence as supportive of his discretionary theory that managers would serve themselves when they weren't closely supervised. That is, where the opportunity for discretion exists, managers will use this discretion to pay themselves more [139, p. 134]. His finding also indicated that the level of salary-plus-bonus income depends significantly on the concentration ratio and barriers-to-entry, even when the firm's profitability was included as an additional explanatory variable. This suggests that compensation studies neglecting inter-industry differences may be omitting some important information.

Williamson conceded that his use of the internal representation-on-the-board variable would be an unbiased predictor of management control only if there were no correlation between the distribution of ownership and internal representation [139, p. 132], but since he lacked data concerning the distribution of shares he was unable to test for such a relationship. (The link between internal representation on a board of directors and the distribution of stock will be examined in the next chapter.)

The other attempt to examine compensation based on the type of control was undertaken by Larner [69]. For a sample of 94 large industrial corporations he used several alternative measures of compensation as the dependent variable and regressed them on several combinations of explanatory variables. These combinations yielded a total of 42 cross-section linear regressions covering the period 1960-1965. He then selected the 76

---

[a] Masson argues that such a problem, if it exists at all, is likely to be short run in nature and is therefore unlikely to affect the manager's compensation scheme over a long period [86, pp. 1290-91]. Of course, whether insiders can predict and act on anticipated success or failure is an empirical question. The manager's ability to exploit information in the short run is carefully circumscribed by law (e.g., see Manne [74]). But there is evidence that insiders do better than average when dealing with their own stock. H.K. Wu found that insiders can generally predict future price movements of shares in their own companies and are able to profit from this information [144].

manager-controlled firms from the sample of 94 firms and ran 42 more regressions using this subsample. Larner thereby produced a voluminous regression analysis taking twelve full pages to display [69, pp. 46-58]. Although it is difficult even to summarize his results, they generally confirm the Lewellen and Huntsman findings that profits do the best job at explaining executive compensation, regardless of the definition of compensation.

Larner was unable to observe any "consistent pattern of major differences" [69, p. 46] between the subsample of 76 manager-controlled firms and the total sample of 94 firms of both control types, but it is not clear what he was testing for, or what he expected to observe. If he wanted to test for differences between owner-controlled and manager-controlled firms there are more sophisticated statistical techniques available than simply making a visual comparison of the manager-controlled group with a sample consisting of both groups. Even if Larner had employed a technique that allowed for a direct comparison of the two groups, he seems to err in grouping firms where the dominant owner is the manager with firms where the dominant owner is not part of management. It is not clear that these two groups can be expected to have similar compensation structure. Larner did not include any term representing the firm's market value but we now know through the studies by Masson and Lewellen and Huntsman that market value can be an important determinant of compensation. And, finally, Larner's definition ignored retirement benefits and we now know, based on Lewellen's work, that this represents a sizable portion of income. In general, Larner has undertaken an ambitious research project—perhaps too ambitious. Rather than look at selective variables he tried averages, first differences, lagged values, and current values for all his explanatory variables. This produced a volume of data that even he appeared to have trouble digesting. He spent less than four pages discussing twelve pages of results, leaving the bulk of the interpretation to the reader.

Summary. In sum, the early empirical work using the salary plus bonus definition of executive income found income to be significantly related to the level of sales, but later work, employing a fuller definition of income, found profits and the firm's market value to be the key explanatory variables with sales insignificant. And even when these later studies used salary-plus-bonus, the sales term was never significant. The reason for the inconsistency in the two results is not entirely clear, but the earlier studies neglected to consider the firm's market value and later research indicates this to be an important determinant of compensation, plus the later studies by Masson [86] and Lewellen and Huntsman [73] were able to reduce the problems of multicollinearity. All of the cross-sectional studies except Williamson's [139] and Roberts' [109] neglected inter-industry differences in compensation although Williamson's results suggest industry factors should be considered.

All of these later studies noted that the sales term was never significant. But if the compensation package is designed to maximize profits and if the manager derives utility from additional sales, *ceteris paribus*, then one might ask: Why shouldn't sales, *ceteris paribus*, be penalized?; and so why shouldn't the sales term show up to be negative? The sales term is negative but not significant in about half the cases in the Lewellen and Huntsman and Larner studies. It is also negative but not significant in Masson's study. The research looking at compensation based on control type was inconclusive, with some suggestion that manager-controlled firms pay their managers more, but the definition of manager-controlled appears questionable.

c. Promotion Incentives

Another way of looking at the structure of managerial incentives is to consider the promotion process. Alchian contends that opportunities will arise within the managerial group for some to gain personally by eliminating other-than-profit maximizing behavior [1, p. 341]. He argues that managers compete for promotions and new jobs by performing well in their present jobs. Hence even in the absence of the stock-market or product-market constraints the manager is motivated to perform in the stockholders' interests because of the incentive for promotion. Marris, to the contrary, contends that promotion comes about by expanding the number of layers in the organization and this results only from firm growth [83, pp. 92-99]. Marris argues that managers are judged for promotion not on their ability to contribute to profits but on how much they add to the firm's expansion. Thus to the extent that there is a promotion incentive, it is perverse.

There is little evidence to support or refute these contentions. An indirect test of these positions might be obtained through an examination of executive mobility. Mobility says little about the promotion criteria within firms, but it may shed light on inter-firm competition for managers. The evidence indicates that managers, particularly top managers, seldom change jobs. Roberts examined 500 corporate executives and found that only one in seven had changed firms since becoming an officer [109, pp. 109-131]. Forty percent of the managers in his sample had only one employer since age twenty-five. Durbrow studied 5,300 executives from ten industries and concluded that mobility had been greatly exaggerated in the literature [36]. Like Roberts, he found an inverse relationship between mobility and years with the firm. Williamson reviewed the top mangement in the ten largest industrial corporations in 1967 [139, p. 303]. None of the presidents and only one board chairman had been selected from outside the company. The median years of employment with the firm was thirty-one years for the board chairmen and twenty-three years for the presidents. This pattern for presidents holds true for vice presidents in the firm as well [139, p. 304]. So there does not appear to be a significant amount of inter-firm executive mobility. This is not surprising in view of the vested nature of much of the top executive's compensation.

An alternative approach to examining job tenure was taken by Robert L. Sorenson, who tried to determine effects due to type of control. He divided firms into manager-controlled and owner-controlled categories to examine differences in turnover rates when both types of firms experienced long-run profit declines [125, p. 185].[b] Sorenson noted that if the top managers in each control category had been equally capable of weathering the period of below-average profits, then one would not expect to observe a difference in the turnover rate of the top managers. But Sorenson found that the rate of turnover in the owner-controlled group was 32 percent versus a rate of 45 percent for the manager-controlled group (and this difference was significant at the 0.05 level). He viewed this as evidence that manager-controlled firms do a better job at policing top management during bad times.[c]

But Sorenson's owner-controlled category included firms that had a dominant stockholder who also served as the firm's top executive together with firms that had a dominant stockholder but hired the top executive. One might expect to observe differences in turnover rates between these two types of firms. Surely a dominant stockholder would be more reluctant to fire himself than a hired manager, for the owner-manager has access to the same stream of pecuniary and nonpecuniary incentives that face the hired manager. It appears that a more appropriate way of viewing turnover rates would be to consider three control categories rather than two: firms with a dominant stockholder and hired manager, firms with a dominant stockholder as manager, and firms without any dominant interest. With this threefold classification system one can examine differences between tenure for the hired manager under a dominant stockholder and tenure for the hired manager without a dominant stockholder.

Empirical studies of the manager's financial incentives have been examined in this section. Although the manager's total income does appear to be tied to the firm's profitability and its market value, it is not clear that the incentives provided by the promotion mechanism, either within firms or through markets, encourage managers to behave strictly in the stockholders' interests.

---

[b] Long-run profit declines were defined as periods of four or more years during which the company experienced a rate of return on equity which was at least one percentage point below its industry average [125, p. 185]. Sorenson's results were reported by Boyle and Hogarty [19].

[c] Louis De Alessi examined executive tenure between government-owned utilities and privately-owned but public-regulated utilities and found that the top executives in the 100 government-owned firms had on average significantly longer tenure than the top executives in the 100 privately-owned firms [32].

Constraints on Managerial Discretion

The examination of the manager's financial incentives was an attempt to answer the Berle and Means query concerning "the degree to which the self interest" of the managers "run parallel to the interest of ownership" [15, p. 113]. A second line of research has been to consider, insofar as the goals of managers and owners differ, the effectiveness of the "checks on the use of power" [15, p. 114]. Berle and Means focused on the check provided by the existence of a dominant stockholding interest and many researchers have attempted to replicate the original study [21; 23; 69; 105; 116; 133]. Others considered the effectiveness of the product-market [3; 12; 41, p. 22; 141] and capital-market constraints [9; 15, p. 247; 34; 54, p. 430; 137], as well as the market for corporate control [15, pp. 82-83; 42, p. 1150; 55; 68; 83; 84, p. 44; 121; 140] in disciplining other-than-profit maximizing behavior by the manager. The literature examining the prevalence of a dominant stockholding interest among large corporations will be discussed in Part a. The product and capital-market constraints, including the market for corporate control, will be examined in Part b.

a. The Dominant Stockholder Constraint

Berle and Means were the first to examine the control conditions prevailing in large industrial corporations [15]. Relying upon trade publications and "street knowledge" of the corporate structure, they attempted to determine the locus of power for the largest 200 nonfinancial corporations during 1929. Defining stockholder control as represented by 20 percent or more of the common stock in the hands of a single party, they found that 44 percent of the firms were under the control of the management [15, p. 109]. They concluded that "control is maintained in large measure apart from ownership" [15, pp. 110-11].

The Securities and Exchange Commission, conducting a study for the Temporary National Economic Committee in 1937, adopted a more rigorous research technique in calculating the 20 largest stockholders in the 200 largest nonfinancial corporations [133]. With a 10 percent stock ownership requirement for control, they concluded that two-thirds of the firms were owned by families or various outside interests [133, p. 104]. Gordon reviewed these findings and found, however, that in less than a third of their sample did "a small compact group of individuals exercise control" [48, p. 43]. And the decline of dominant ownership interests and gain of management control has been well documented. Larner replicated the Berle and Means study using 1963 data, drawn from individual proxy statements published by the firms [69]. He dropped the ownership requirement for control from 20 percent to 10 percent and found nevertheless that the extent of management control had climbed dramatically from 44 percent in 1929 to 84 percent in 1963. John Palmer adopted Larner's definitions and calculated this figure to be 88 percent in 1969 [105]. John Sheehan found that in 1966 a single individual, or the members of a single family, owned 10 percent or more of the voting stock in about 150 of the Fortune 500 firms [116, p. 178]. But only eleven of the top 100 firms were so controlled.

Philip Burch, in a recent monograph [21], criticized earlier research because be felt that the formal reporting procedure on stock holdings would tend to underestimate the prevalence of a dominant stock-holding interest. Relying primarily on references drawn from various magazines and newspapers, he reconstructed the control status of the top 500 nonfinancial corporations as of 1965 and found nearly twice the number of owner-controlled firms as found by Larner. But his methodology for classifying firms appears arbitrary. For example, he had no clearly defined minimum stockholding requirements for classifying firms as owner-controlled. A firm was classified as owner-controlled if "one or more family names appear frequently in the upper managerial echelons" [21, pp. 18-19], regardless of the pattern of stock distribution. Burch questioned the Berle and Means analysis for its use of "street knowledge," but he seems to resort to a very similar approach. And in spite of the higher prevalence of owner-controlled firms found by Burch, he does agree with earlier studies that the trend is towards management control. In comparing the top 100 firms in his work with the top 100 in the 1937 TNEC study, he noted that 50 percent of the firms in the earlier study were owner-controlled whereas only 36 percent of his top 100 were so controlled [21, p. 104].

Although the above studies do not agree on the exact fraction required for control, all concede that the control in the largest corporations is passing from the dominant stockholder. Death and taxes appear to work against the perpetuation of the family firm. Managerial control of the large corporation has become generally accepted in the literature as part of the "conventional wisdom" [13, pp. 70-74; 14; 92]. But not all believe that control has passed to the managers. Paul Sweezy argues that the old capitalist families have transferred their ownership and active participation out of the large corporation into financial institutions, primarily banks, through which they continue to dominate the affairs not only of corporations but of other financial interests as well [129].[d] And Gabriel Kolko contends that large stockholders conceal their identity by placing their stocks in professionally managed trusts and investment companies [67, p. 62].

A few studies have considered the holdings of institutional investors in

---

[d] J.C. Knowles in an attempt to support this contention has traced out the holdings of the "Rockefeller Financial Group" [61].

examining control. Don Villarejo included the holdings of investment companies and insurance companies in his definition of control [135]. He relied upon TNEC data along with the SEC's *Official Summary* to examine the 250 top industrial corporations in 1959. Using a 5 percent control requirement and aggregating the holdings of investment companies, insurance companies, and the board of directors, he concluded that from one-half to three-fifths of the firms were owner-controlled. Since he derived control by aggregating the holdings of the three groups, this definition assumes that the directors, investment companies, and insurance companies all behave as a single dominant force. Since there is no evidence that this is the case, this classification scheme does not appear to be clearly justified. Moreover he neglects the holdings of the largest institutional stockholders, the commercial banks.

Jean-Marie Chevalier considered the holdings of large commercial banks in her calculations of control in the 200 largest firms in 1965 [23]. She adopted a 5 percent ownership requirement and found that only about 40 percent of these firms were manager-controlled. In 26 instances out of 200, the trust departments of the giant banks had holdings large enough to be considered as minority controllers, or as having a "dominant influence." In 18 of these 26 cases control was based on the bank's holdings of various corporate pension funds [23, p. 168]. To observe the trend in bank holdings over time, Chevalier compared the 85 firms common to both her study and the TNEC study and found that control by banks and by management both increased between 1937 and 1965. Again the individual dominant stockholders lost ground over the period.

Institutional holdings are clearly on the rise. Holdings by the trust departments of banks, mutual funds, insurance companies, and nonprofit organizations were estimated to be about 30 percent outstanding common shares in 1968, more than twice as high as in 1949.[e] The Morgan Guaranty Trust Company alone recently held over 7 percent of the common stock in three major airlines [46, p. 13]. The Fidelity Management and Research Corporation held over 5 percent of the common stock in 27 large corporations [16, p. 139]. Although the institutions have the potential for control, whether they can function as the dominant stockholder of old is still an open issue. Indeed, it is not yet clear whether a large bank can legally wield its financial power. For example, the Justice Department recently sued the Cleveland Trust Company, charging it with substantially lessening competition in the machine tool industry by holding in trust large blocks of stock in four firms in that industry [57, p. 67]. Consequently, institutional investors may tend to be more cautious in selecting their portfolio and using their

---

[e] Pension funds alone accounted for 7 percent of the common stock in 1965 [23, p. 87]. Wrightsman predicted that given the current trend, this figure will be 23.3 percent by 1980 [142; 143]. Pension funds have been adding more stock to their portfolio than any other class of investor. See also the study by the House Banking and Finance Committee [132].

power. Yet even if institutions simply sell their shares rather than attempt to reform an inefficient manager, they are thereby registering their disapproval of the firm's policies, and contributing to the efficiency of the market for corporate control.

Some years ago Berle suggested that a firm went through four stages of corporate control: (1) absolute stockholder control, which is private ownership or majority control; (2) working or minority control; (3) management control; and finally, (4) control by financial institutions through which dispersed stock holdings once more became concentrated [13]. Although management control may be the most common condition found in the above studies, many large firms in the economy appear to be heading for Berle's fourth stage.

b. The Market for Corporate Control

Several economists have noted that even with the change in the nature of corporate ownership the "economics of natural selection" will ensure that only the most efficient firms survive [3; 12; 41, p. 22]. The forces of competition in the product market will not permit the manager to stray far from the norm of profit maximization if the firm is to remain viable. In rebutting this argument, Sidney Winter has shown that the product-market discipline is not an effective constraint in market situations involving market power [141]. In view of Winter's argument it is no surprise that all of the discretionary theories of the firm assume not only the separation of ownership from control, but a lack of strict competition in the product market.

Given that the dominant-stockholder and product-market constraints are relaxed, what other constraints does the manager face? Berle and Means spent a great deal of time discrediting the effectiveness of the legal instruments, such as the derivative suit and the proxy contest, at the disposal of all stockholders [15, Bk. II], which will not be explicitly dealt with in this study. The only check that Berle and Means attached any weight to is the manager's need for a steady flow of capital:

Only one general protection besides the power of active revolt remains to guarantee a measure of equitable treatment to the several classes of security holders. The enterprise may need new capital. The management must, therefore, maintain a situation in which additional capital is forthcoming [15, p. 247].

This is similar to the constraint employed by Baumol thirty years later [8]. The firm with poor profitability prospects will reflect a lower share price, making it more difficult for the firm to grow by raising additional funds in the capital market.

There appear to be some serious shortcomings with such a constraint. For one thing, evidence shows that large firms resort to the capital market only infrequently.[f] But even if the capital market were relied on more heavily, John Williamson's analysis has shown that growth will not be limited by the lack of finance alone [137, p. 3]. Brian Hindley noted that it is always possible to raise revenue by sellling additional shares. The price of the share may drop in the process, but this simply represents a transfer of wealth from present to future stockholders [54, p. 430]. Even Baumol admits that "the stock market is only infrequently given the opportunity to discipline directly the vast majority of the nation's leading corporations . . ." [10, p. 83]. Thus the capital market, in its role of limiting the source of new capital, does not appear to be an effective constraint on managerial behavior.

But the capital market can play a more vital role in disciplining various forms of inefficiency. As Alchian and Kessel point out, the capital market will allocate monopoly rights to those that can use them most profitably [4, p. 160]. The manager who sacrifices profits for other objectives, and thereby allows the value of the firm's shares to slip, opens his firm to a possible take-over by an outsider interested in buying shares at the depressed level and experiencing capital gains after imposing corporate reforms. This market mechanism is the primary constraint on managerial behavior in the Marris model [83]. The effectiveness of this constraint has been a much debated issue in recent years. Henry Manne feels, "the market for corporate control serves an extraordinary important purpose in the functioning of the corporate system" [80, p. 112]. J.E. Meade notes: "A company which sacrifices profit either to an easy life or to an unprofitable growth makes itself liable to a takeover bid. . . Experience suggests that large companies are in fact threatened with this fate if they fail to be sufficiently profit-minded" [89, p. 387]. Robert Solow also relies upon the take-over bid to ensure that the management will not "freely sacrifice profits for growth," but, he concedes, "the very largest corporations are not subject to this threat . . ." [124, p. 107].

Not all view the market for corporate control as an effective constraint. Berle and Means mentioned it and even provided examples, but they discounted its effectiveness [15, pp. 82-83]. O.E Williamson feels that if such a market exists, transaction costs are high and actions to alter control can be largely insensitive to sizable fluctuations in the price of the share [140, p. 317]. Even Marris, who posits the take-over mechanism as the primary constraint on management, feels that over time the process of

---

[f] Donaldson studied the financing of 20 large U.S. firms for the twenty-year period 1939-1958. He found that 50 percent of the firms never resorted to equity financing during the period, 25 percent did only once, and the remaining 25 percent did two or three times. With debt financing included, 62 percent of the firms generated over 95 percent of their funds internally and only three firms fell below 80 percent [34].

selection will drive out those who maximize profits and leave only those who maximize growth: "Since the growth oriented managements will by definition be located in the faster growing corporations, this type of behavior must in time drive out other types. . . . The further this process goes the weaker is the power of the stock market to resist" [84, p. 44]. In the final analysis, the question concerning the effectiveness of the market for corporate control is an empirical one. The assumption that the separation of ownership from control along with imperfect product markets affords the manager an opportunity to divert a significant amount of potential profits to his own ends is based on the notion that the transaction costs in the market for corporate control are very high relative to the potential value of a controlling interest. These costs have not been examined directly,[g] but three researchers have taken an indirect approach by comparing the properties of those firms that had been subject to a take-over with those that had not [55; 68; 121].

Brian Hindley made use of the Marris valuation ratio (the ratio of a firm's market value to its net asset value) as an index of efficiency to compare firms that had experienced contests for control between 1958 and 1963 with uncontested firms in the same industry [55, p. 187]. He relied upon the value of the firm's net assets as a proxy for the firm's potential value. After testing to see whether the 49 contested firms had significantly lower valuation ratios than groups of uncontested firms in the same industry, he concluded that corporations that had been subject to intervention displayed valuation ratios that were lower than the industry average, suggesting that an active market for corporate control did exist [55, p. 201]. But at the same time he found a sizable number of firms that had larger than average differentials between their actual and potential value, and yet had not been acquisition targets. He therefore concluded that the market for corporate control was partially ineffective [55, p. 220]. D.A. Kuehn found similar results in a study of 250 U.K. quoted companies [68]. Using a dummy variable for firms that were taken over, his results indicated that corporations were more likely to be subjected to a take-over bid if the market value of their common stock had been depressed relative to net assets [68, p. 44]. Yet his overall explanatory power was quite low.

The most ambitious study concerning the market for corporate control was carried out by Agit Singh [121]. Beginning with 2,000 British industrial firms quoted on the stock exchange in 1954, he found that about 400 had been taken over or had disappeared through merger by the end of 1960. He

---
[g]The closest piece to a direct study is by S.L. Hayes and R.A. Taussig [51], who looked at the premium paid for tender offers. If control is acquired by a tender offer, part of the acquisition cost consists of the premium above the going price of the share that must be offered to attract a sufficient number of shares. Hayes and Taussig examined the difference between the market price and the offer price and found "the median premiums offered by bidders was 16 percent over the market price two days before the offer" with premiums ranging from zero to 44 percent [51, p. 140].

compared the financial characteristics of the taken-over firms with the other firms. He also compared acquiring firms with non-acquiring firms. Ten basic variables were used to describe the record of each firm. In general Singh's results indicate that the stock market, through the market for corporate control, was a rather imperfect disciplinarian, particularly with respect to medium-sized and large firms. The market appeared to be more effective for small firms. For example, the data suggest that small firms with below-average profit records were able to decrease their chances of acquisition simply by raising the rate of profit above the industry average. But for medium-sized and large firms with below-average profits, the best way to reduce the probability of a take-over might have been to increase their size rather than their profits. As Singh noted: "In general it appears possible for the medium sized and large firms to maintain their rate of profit, or even lower it, and yet increase their chances of survival, provided they can achieve a sufficient increase in size" [121, p. 152]. Although these conclusions appear to be speculative, they suggest that rather than disciplining growth maximization, the market for corporate control may actually encourage it, at least among medium-sized to large firms.

Singh examined the typical acquiring firm, and found it to be "a large, dynamic firm with a very high rate of growth" [121, p. 166]. It was significantly more profitable than the average acquired firm, but not more profitable than the average non-acquiring firm. There was too much overlap between the acquired firms and surviving firms for Singh to sort them out, but profitability appeared to be the most useful variable here.

The empirical work on the market for corporate control is inconclusive. It appears that a market for corporate control exists but there is some question as to its sensitivity or the overall impact that it has in constraining other-than-profit-maximizing behavior. One problem the three studies face is that the more sensitive the market for control is, the more difficult it will be to observe differences between firms subjected to a take-over and firms not subjected to a take-over. It is only when the transaction costs of control are high that large "discrepancies" will be observed between the two classes of firms. If no significant difference exists between acquired an non-acquired firms one cannot conclude that the market for corporate control does not exist; this may mean the market is so sensitive it responds to differences that elude the crude measures used by researchers.

The Effects of the Separation of Ownership from Control

Rather than focus on the manager's incentives and constraints another approach has been to focus on the control condition of the firm to see whether the separation of ownership from control has any impact on managerial performance. Nearly all studies of this latter type sort firms into either owner-controlled or manager-controlled categories[h] and proceed to examine differences in various performance characteristics such as rate of return [17; 57; 60; 61; 69; 90; 103; 108; 125], firm risk [17; 61; 101], and the firm's retention policy [58; 125; 139]. This procedure is actually an indirect test of the effectiveness of the other incentives and constraints on the manager. If no significant difference is observed between control types, it is interpreted as evidence that in the absence of a dominant interest the manager is motivated by other forces to behave as if he were under the influence of a dominant interest.

All of this literature is quite recent and has not been brought together elsewhere. Consequently, each piece will be discussed in some detail with comparisons among results drawn where possible. Critical comments which are common to all studies will be held until the end of each subsection. The effect of the type of control on the firm's rate of return will be examined first, followed by a discussion of risk and the retention policy.

Type of Control and the Rate of Return

Until the spring of 1968 there were no published studies examining differences in firms' profitability due to the type of control that prevailed in them. Since then there have been at least five doctoral dissertations [57; 61; 69; 103; 125] plus several research articles [17; 60; 90; 108] relating the firm's rate of return to a type-of-control variable. All differ in certain respects, either in the sample selected, the statistical approach, the definition of control, or the additional explanatory variables employed, but a few of the studies are quite similar and these similarities will be noted.

Two studies appearing in the spring of 1968 attempted to determine if manager-controlled firms had lower rates of return on equity than owner-controlled firms [60; 90]. Although the two studies seemed to be approaching the test in the same general way, the results, at first, appear to be quite different. David Kamerschen concluded that his type-of-control variable "does not appear to explain very much of the variation in profit rates among the 200 largest non-financial corporations" [60, pp. 445-46]. But

---

[h] Empirical researchers have defined owner-controlled firms as firms having a dominant stockholder, either as a manager or outside the firm, who owns enough stock to exercise effective control over the firm. However, the theoretical studies use varying, and less explicit, definitions of control. Gordon distinguished between firms headed by an "owner-enterpriser" and firms headed by a "professional manager" [48, p. 322]. Baumol spoke of "nonowner-operated" firms [9, p. 103], implying that the remaining firms must be owner-operated firms. Monsen and Downs initially distinguished between "owner-managed firms" and "concentrated ownership managerial firms," in addition to "diffused ownership managerial firms" [92, p. 223], but, they argued, the first two are "nearly identical" [92, p 223].

R.J. Monsen, J.S. Chiu, and D.E. Cooley found that "owner controlled firms provide a much better return on the original investment . . ." [90, p. 442]. Kamerschen used Larner's sample [69] consisting of the 200 largest nonfinancial corporations based on assets in 1963. This sample included transportation firms and regulated utilities.[i] Monsen et al. limited their selection to industrial firms because of "the variations in accounting techniques and other incomparabilities" [90, p. 436] if other types of firms were used. Since preliminary research suggested that the profit rate was strongly related to the industry, they choose three owner-controlled firms and three manager-controlled firms from each of twelve industries, with all selections drawn from the top 500 industrial firms, based on sales.

The dependent variable in each study was the ratio of firms' net income to net worth. Kamerschen considered the average rate of return from 1959 to 1964, but Monsen et al. used annual observations between 1952 and 1963. Both utilized a type of control dummy variable but the definition of control differed.[j] Kamerschen employed nine additional explanatory variables primarily to account for inter-industry differences. Since Monsen et al. selected their sample based on the industry their only additional terms were a size of firm variable plus industry and time dummy variables.

Kamerschen divided his sample into four subsamples depending upon the availability of data for his explanatory variable. He reported on only the sample using 47 firms and found his control variable "is always statistically insignificant" [60, p. 445] at the 0.05 level. But he applied a two-tailed test, though he cited the "new theories" as suggesting that *"ceteris paribus*, managerial-controlled firms presumably would be less concerned with profit maximization" [60, p. 435] than owner-controlled firms. Therefore, he appeared to be testing the hypothesis that manager-controlled firms have lower profit rates, suggesting that a one-tailed test would be appropriate. With a one-tailed test his type of control variable actually would be significant at the 0.05 level four of the seven times it appeared. In the three instances where it was not significant, the growth rate of the firm had been introduced as an additional explanatory variable. As one might suspect,

---

[i] Kamerschen's inclusion of regulated utilities is troublesome. Since the rate of return in these firms is dictated by a regulatory body and prices are set accordingly, the control condition would not appear to matter as much, since even the more "inefficient" firm can show a "normal" rate of return by adjusting its rate structure. About one-third of Kamerschen's sample consisted of regulated firms. Including such firms in the sample would appear to make it more difficult to observe any difference in profitability based on the control type.

[j] Kamerschen used Larner's 10 percent criterion [69] and thereby sorted all firms in the top 200 into one category or another. Monsen et al. selected their sample more carefully and obtained firms only from the extremes of the control distribution. Owner-controlled firms were defined as having one party owning at least 10 percent and was known to control or one party owning 20 percent of the voting stock, whereas manager-controlled firms had no single party exceeding 5 percent with no evidence of recent control [90, pp. 438-39]. In effect, Monsen et al. tested a weaker hypothesis that a difference could be observed between two extreme control conditions.

subsequent analysis of his sample in another study revealed that the control variable and the rate of growth variable were significantly related [59, p. 491]. Owner-controlled firms grew at a faster rate.

Another explanatory variable, which Kamerschen regarded as important, was a dummy variable for those firms that had experienced a change in the type of control between 1929 and 1963. He noted that in most instances the change in control was from owner-controlled to manager-controlled. He found these firms to be significantly more profitable than firms that had not experienced a change of control, and other authors as well as Kamerschen have used this evidence as an argument against the hypothesis that manager-controlled firms are less profitable.[k] The implication they draw is that firms were more profitable because they had experienced a change in control, but the relevant question is: How did their current profitability compare with profitability before the change in control? These firms may well have been even more profitable in the past and dropped only after the managers came into power. Kamerschen's cross-sectional observation about an intrinsically time-series phenomenon is therefore unhelpful, and it could even be misleading.

After carefully selecting their sample of owner-controlled and manager-controlled firms and after taking size, industry, and time into account, Monsen et al. found that the owner-controlled group was significantly more profitable at the 0.0005 level. In an appendix they collapsed the twelve annual observations into an average profit rate for each firm and found that the control variable was still significant but only at the 0.08 level. (Note the degrees of freedom and significance levels were inflated by examining the same firm over a period of twelve years.) This collapsed version is similar to Kamerschen's approach, since average profitability is examined in each case, although the samples were chosen according to different definitions for control.

Thus the results do not appear to differ as much as one might surmise from the authors' concluding remarks. Since Kamerschen sorted all of the top 200 firms into one control group or another he actually was testing a stronger hypothesis. Monsen et al. were much more careful in their selection procedure, omitting any firm from the sample which did not clearly fall in one well-defined group or another. Aside from the irregularities associated with including regulated industries in the sample, it might be

---

[k] J.V. Koch, for example, says Kamerschen found "that changes in control from owner-controlled to manager-controlled status for a given firm was associated with increased profit rates" [66, p. 38] . F.M. Sherer makes similar comments noting this is the "opposite of what one might anticipate on *a priori* grounds" [112, p. 34]. An example of the confusion on this point is expressed by the following quote from H.K. Radice appearing in the *Economic Journal*:

[Kamerschen] split his sample into those firms which remained owner-controlled in 1963 as in 1929, those which remained management-controlled, and those which changed from the former to the latter. Of the three groups, the owner-controlled groups had the lowest profit rates [108, p. 559].

argued that Kamerschen's results are more convincing in favor of a difference due to control than the Monsen et al. results, partly because his sampling procedure was less arbitrary. Nevertheless, industry-related variables appear to be quite important and comparing firms in the same industry is preferable to looking at all firms and then attempting to account for inter-industry differences.

Leon P. Jorgensen recently came very close to duplicating Kamerschen's work [57]. He drew upon Kamerschen's sample, including utilities, so the same reservations concerning the use of regulated firms in a study of this type apply here as well. He used all of Kamerschen's data but changed the average profit term from the 1959-1964 time period to the 1958-1963 time period. He introduced two additional type-of-control variables: a variable representing the internal composition of the board of directors, and a variable expanding Larner's definition of control to include the stock holdings of large commercial banks. After regressing several combinations of independent variables he concluded that his results do not suggest that the manager-controlled group is less profitable, or less efficient, than the non-management group [57, p. 76].[1] It seems odd that Jorgensen's results differ from Kamerschen's since he uses a similar sample and comparable statistical procedures. His adjusted coefficient of determination is consistently about one-half that derived by Kamerschen. It is likely that Jorgensen, like Kamerschen, has collinearity between the type of control and the growth variable.

Just as Jorgensen duplicated Kamerschen's research, Kenneth J. Boudreaux's work [17] is quite similar to the Monsen et al. study. Although there is no mention of the similarities in his analysis, he used the same twelve industries, the same twelve year period (1952-63), the same control criteria, and the same statistical methodology as the Monson et al. study. The only difference in the two samples is that eight of the 72 firms in each sample differ.[m] Like the Monsen et al. collapsed version, he employed an analysis of variance model to uncover differences in average profitability based on control type. He concluded that "owner-controlled firms exhibit higher rates of return," which he deemed supportive of earlier findings, including the Monsen et al. results [17, p. 370]. Since Boudreaux's approach is identical to the Monsen et al. collapsed version, the F-values found in Boudreaux's table 2 [17, p. 368] can be compared with the F-values

---

[1] Neither the Larner measure of control nor the revised measure with bank holdings is significant for the two samples he looks at ($N = 200$, $N = 67$), but his internal representation variable indicates for the large sample that firms with a higher proportion of managers on the board are more profitable. Jorgensen was puzzled by this result, noting that this is the opposite of the sign predicted by the new theories. This point will be discussed in Chapter 5.

[m] By comparing Boudreaux's published appendix [17, pp. 372-73] with an unpublished appendix to the Monsen et al. study [91], the two samples can be analyzed. Six of the 36 manager-controlled firms and two of the 36 owner-controlled firms differ between the two samples. The differences between the two samples when measuring risk will be discussed below.

found in table 3 [90, p. 446] of the Monsen et al. study. The control variable in the latter study has an F-value of 3.23 and this is significant at the 0.08 level, but the control variable in Boudreaux's study has an F-value of 13.84 and this is significant at the 0.001 level. Thus in spite of the fact that only eight of the seventy-two firms differ between the two samples, Boudreaux's significance levels are sharply higher. If the Monsen et al. study can be faulted because of arbitrariness in the firm selection procedure, the Boudreaux study is even more exposed to criticism, since he appears to have made substitutions in the Monsen et al. sample. At least these procedures would appear to require further explanation before results based on them can be accepted.

Boudreaux next introduced risk and size as continuous explanatory variables and, using an analysis of covariance, found that the type of control still remains significant but at the 0.05 rather than the 0.001 level. The risk term (the standard deviation of profit rates over the twelve-year period) was positively and significantly related to profit rates at the 0.05 level. Firm size was positive and significant at the 0.10 level [17, p. 369]. Another objective of Boudreaux's study was to look at the risk or variability of the firm's profit stream based on the control condition. This aspect of his work will be discussed in the next section.

A dissertation by Philip Karst examined the link between the holdings of the board of directors and performance of the firm for a sample of about twenty firms in each of two industries [61]. He concluded that the larger the fraction of the firm held by members of the board of directors, the higher the profit level and the greater the returns to stockholders. Karst is one of the few who attempted to develop his own theoretical framework for his tests, so a brief discussion of his analysis is in order. (The following is a brief summary from Chapters III and IV [61].) In his model the manager produces net revenues which he converts into either discretionary expenditures or reported profits. Karst viewed discretionary expenditures (similar to Williamson's emoluments term) as the main reason why managers without an ownership interest wish to produce net revenue. If the firm is under the control of a dominant stockholder not on the board of directors, this dominant interest is able to police discretionary expenditures so the manager has little incentive to produce net revenue. Consequently, the manager will be more lax and net revenue will be relatively low. The manager in the absence of a dominant outside interest has an incentive to produce net revenue since he can convert some (or all?) into discretionary expenditures. As the manager's holdings in the firm increase, he is more able to share in reported profits, so he has more incentive to turn net revenue into reported profits.

To test his model Karst used the fraction of the firm held by the board of directors as his measure of managerial holdings in the firm. This measure seems inappropriate, however, for the directors that are not part of management have little access to the flow of discretionary expenditures. Non-managing directors would appear to have the same incentives to eliminate discretionary expenditures as the outside controller. Thus if the stock were entirely in the hands of outside directors one should expect a different outcome than if that same amount were in the hands of the managers. Yet Karst's theoretical formulation does not distinguish between the two situations. As far as the outsider's ability to police discretionary expenditures is concerned, it seems a bit strained to assume the outsider can track down this type of activity and yet is powerless if the manager decides that he doesn't want to produce profits. Why not fire him? Or at least tie his income to his performance? Karst seems to ignore the body of literature linking the manager's income to the profitability and the market value of the firm.

John Palmer has undertaken what appears to be the most imaginative study dealing with the effects of the separation of ownership from control [103]. His is one of the few studies to consider the product market constraint as well as the separation issue in forming a dual constraint on managerial behavior. His dependent variable was the average rate of return on net worth from 1961 to 1965 and from 1966 to 1969 for each of the 500 largest industrial corporations. His three explanatory variables were the type-of-control, the monopoly power of the firm, and the size of the firm. He defined a firm as strong-owner-controlled if one party owned 30 percent or more of the firm's common stock, weak-owner-controlled, between 10 percent and 30 percent, and manager-controlled otherwise [103, p. 294]. A barriers-to-entry term was used to estimate monopoly power, and total sales represented firm size. He found, as did Hall and Weiss [50], a negative relationship between firm size and the variance of profit rates, presumably due to sampling effects in large firms. To avoid the heteroscedasticity which would arise in regression analysis he compared subsamples by size categories rather than using regression analysis. He compared the average reported profit rates for his three types of control, holding monopoly power constant, and concluded that only among firms with a high degree of monopoly power was there a significant difference based on the type of control [103, p. 298].

Palmer's results are interesting for emphasis on the dual nature of the constraint on management. Previous studies neglected the product market constraint and considered size per se as sufficient grounds for monopoly power. Palmer showed that when barriers to entry are relatively low the managers in each control situation have similar returns. Only when the product market constraint is relaxed is there a divergence in profitability based on the control type.

Robert Larner drew upon the original Hall and Weiss sample to select a group of 128 management-controlled and 59 owner-controlled firms [69]. The annual profit rate between 1956 and 1962 was the dependent variable with a control dummy, a series of terms to account for inter-industry market conditions, a time dummy, and the equity/asset ratio as explanatory variables [69, p. 30]. Like Palmer, he also found that the variability of profits was smaller for large firms. To satisfy the homoscedasticity assumption for regression analysis he adjusted his data, as had Hall and Weiss [50], by multiplying all variables by the square root of the firm's assets. His final results indicated that profit rates were significantly lower at the 0.05 level in the manager-controlled group; the magnitude of this difference, however, was less than one percentage point [69, p. 31].

H.K. Radice examined the profitability based on control type for a total of 89 British firms in three two-digit industries [108]. He selected his sample carefully to focus on extreme control conditions, with owner-controlled firms having a 15 percent requirement and manager-controlled firms having a 5 percent or less requirement [108, p. 550]. His dependent variable was the average rate of return between 1957 and 1966, and his explanatory variables were the type of control and industry dummies plus firm size and firm growth. Like Kamerschen, he used a two-tailed test, even though he clamined to be testing the "new" theories [108, p. 552]. which predicted that owner-controlled firms would be more profitable. He found that his control variable was not significant at the 0.05 level either time it appeared. But a one-tailed test seems more appropriate here; and with a one-tailed test the owner-controlled group was significantly more profitable at the 0.05 level both times it appeared [108, p. 559]. When the sample was broken into subsamples by industry, the results were not as clear. The textile industry still had a significant control term but in the food and electrical engineering industries the control term was not significant. By selecting industries which appeared to be relatively competitive, Radice was actually posing a stronger test, yet his results for the entire sample confirm the greater profitability of the owner-controlled group.

The most recent study to appear [126] examining the relationship between control type and firm performance was drawn from research by Robert L. Sorenson [125]. Following the sample selection procedure adopted by Monsen et al. [90], Sorenson selected a total of 30 owner-controlled and 30 manager-controlled firms from eleven industries. An ownership concentration of 20 percent or more qualified the firm as owner-controlled; if no interest owned 5 percent or more of the firm, the firm was defined as manager-controlled [126, p. 146]. Sorenson examined several performance characteristics of the firm including its rate of return to equity and the rate of return on stock purchased in 1948 and held until 1966. He employed an analysis of covariance for each individual industry but neglected to test for differences in control type for the whole sample after accounting for inter-industry differences in performance. Based on his findings for the individual industries, he concluded that owner-controlled firms appeared to earn higher rates of return, but with a difference that was not significant [126, p. 147].

There are two shortcomings with Sorenson's analysis: (1) although he examines the differences based on the control type for individual industries, he neglects to consider the overall effect of control in the full sample of all firms once these inter-industry differences have been accounted for; and (2) although he correctly notes that the "new" theories he cites (Baumol [9], Monsen and Downs [92], and Williamson [139]) assume that to exercise discretion the manager must be "insulated from effective owner control" [126, p. 145], he fails to point out in his discussion or consider in his empirical analysis that the "new" theories also assume that the firms have some non-trivial amount of market power.[n] The first shortcoming overlooks the possibility of more powerful statistical tests of the effect-of-control hypothesis, a matter which is especially important in any claim that there is no effect. The second shortcoming fails to distinguish carefully the circumstances in which the hypothesis is relevant and can interfere with a sound test, for if the manager faces strict competition in the product market, that will constrain his discretionary powers even in the absence of owner-control.

Since Sorenson displayed his data for mean values based on control type in each industry [126, p. 147, table I], he provides us enough information to perform some additional tests. A test designed to examine differences in paired observations such as those provided by Sorenson is the Wilcoxon signed rank test [99, pp. 115-19]. In order to take into account the role of the product market as a constraint on managerial discretion, however, each industry in Sorenson's sample was first examined using H.M. Mann's [78] and W.G. Shepherd's [117, Appendix table 13, pp. 274-81] definitions of barriers to entry. The only industry so to be defined unambiguously as having "moderate to low" barriers to entry was the textile and mill products industry, the remaining industries all possessing some degree of entry barrier.[o] Since the new theories do not claim that the alternative

---

[n] Baumol's analysis is cast explicitly in an oligopolistic environment [9]. Monsen and Downs assume the firms in their model "can usually earn profits larger than the 'normal' level" [92, p. 124], and Williamson considers managers in market situations "where competitive conditions are not typically severe and where the management may therefore enjoy significant discretion in developing its strategy" [139, p. 39].

[o] Certain industries had four digit SIC components which have been defined as having entry barriers ranging from "moderate to low" to "very high." Sorenson's sample of firms for the two digit food and kindred products industry included both meat packing firms with "moderate to low" entry barriers and distilled liquor firms with "very high" entry barriers. Although Sorenson argues that comparing firms in the same industry "is tantamount to holding structure constant" [126, p. 146], this argument appears thin when the industry definition is broad enough to include both meat packing and distilled liquors.

theories of the firm apply in those firms facing strict competition in the product market, the textile and mill products industry was dropped from the sample and the Wilcoxon signed rank test was applied using the mean values by control type in each industry (a total of ten pairs). The results using a one-tailed test indicate that the owner-controlled firms have significantly higher rates of return to equity at the 0.032 level, and have significantly higher rates of return on stock purchased and held over the period at the 0.024 level. When the textile and mill products industry is included in the sample the returns on a share of stock still are significantly higher for the owner-controlled group (at the 0.042 level). All of these results are within the 0.05 level of significance established by Sorenson to test for differences within industries. Although Sorenson concluded that the "separation of ownership and control has not led to substantial differences in firm performance" [126, pp. 147-48], this conclusion appears misleading in view of the above findings using Sorenson's own data.

Summary. Thus of the nine studies we have reviewed, our analysis indicates that eight found owner-controlled firms to be significantly more profitable, with profit rate differences ranging from one-half of a percentage point [69] to over six percentage points [90]. The only study not to observe a difference used essentially the same data as Kamerschen, but failed to confirm his results [57]. The bulk of the studies considered only the dominant stockholder constraint, neglecting the product market. But Palmer has shown that the control condition is likely to make more difference when the product market constraint is relaxed because of the existance of monopoly power.

Although the Hall and Weiss study relating profitability to firm size found that the variability of profits decreased as firm size increased [50], only the Palmer and Larner studies attempted to adjust for heteroscedasticity. If heteroscedasticity also were present in the other studies, estimates derived by those studies were unbiased but not the most efficient, and statistical tests could be biased. However, heteroscedasticity here does not appear to present the problems it usually does.[p]

There are three basic identification problems which appear unavoidable with these types of control studies. The first problem, brought up earlier in discussing Masson's paper [86], involves the direction of the causality: Are

---

[p]Theil notes that the ordinary least square estimation procedure underestimates the true variance of the coefficients only when the error variance moves in the same direction as the magnitude of an explanatory variable. But if the error variance decreases as the explanatory variable increases (in this instance, size) then the OLS estimates yield variances that may overestimate the true variance [131, pp. 247-49]. This would tend to make it more difficult to find significant coefficients if an adjustment for heteroscedasticity is not made. Consequently the studies that found the control variable to be significant, but failed to adjust for heteroscedasticity, are not necessarily misleading. They could underestimate the significance of the control variable, although it must be remembered that they also could overestimate it.

firms more profitable because they are owner-controlled or are they owner-controlled because they are more profitable? For example, one study looked at the holdings of the board of directors and found that in those firms with a higher fraction of holdings, the firms were more profitable and yielded a better return to stockholders [61]. The implication drawn is that the firms perform better because of the larger ownership interest, whereas an alternative hypothesis might argue directors own a larger fraction of the firm because they expect the firm to perform better than other choices they face in the stock market. Because of inside information, directors are more likely to buy into firms that have promise. With the widespread use of stock options managers don't even need inside information; they need not exercise their options until the market reflects the firm's potential. Likewise directors will not buy into firms that they think have poor prospects. And managers are not likely to exercise options if the option price is above the market price. Consequently, to the extent that the director's knowledge of the industry and firm allows him to make better than average decisions in buying and selling shares in his own firm, then the link between the fraction of the firm owned by insiders and the firm's performance will be reinforced.

Moreover, the capital-gain tax is structured so as to encourage dominant stockholders to retain holdings in the more successful firms. Since the capital-gain tax can be avoided entirely if the shares are held and passed on at death, the more successful the firm is and the greater the appreciation in the shares value, then the larger the tax is that can be avoided by holding the shares until death. But the dominant owner with a less successful firm has less incentive to tie up a presumably large fraction of his total portfolio in that firm.

A third but related problem concerning these profitability studies has been raised by De Alessi [33]. He notes that firms which favor new issue to debt and retained earnings will show both an increase in management control and a decrease in the ratio of net income to net worth. Hence, the type of control studies finding owner-controlled firms more profitable may simply be reflecting differences in the financial structure of the two types of firms [33, p. 846]. De Alessi's comments are interesting but they could be better aimed, since financing an expansion out of either new issues *or* retained earnings will have the same impact on the net income to net worth ratio; both new equity and retained earnings become part of net worth. De Alessi's comments might be reworded to say that firms which favor new issues *and* retained earnings to the use of debt will show both an increase in management control and a decrease in the ratio of net income to net worth. This revised statement is more testable; the firm's debt-equity ratio based on the type of control (and adjusting for factors such as industry type) may yield information concerning debt preferences based on control type. Only one study explicitly looked at leverage based on the type of control, and the results did not support De Alessi's contentions that owner-controlled firms are likely to make more use of debt. (Robert Ware found that manager-controlled firms had higher debt-equity ratios for a sample of firms in the food industry [136].) De Alessi's remarks underscore as well the problems of looking at profitability without considering risk, which will be examined in the following section.

There is reason to believe that any examination of differences in profitability between firms is apt to understate the true differences. Although their research was not addressed to differences in profitability based on the type of control, Hall and Weiss point out several reasons why a cross-section analysis of profit differences between firms may be biased downward [50]. Most of the sources of bias concern the more profitable firms: (1) the most profitable firms have incentives for tax purposes to understate their true profits; (2) to the extent that managers view retained earnings as a source of utility, managers may want to understate true profits so as not to appear to be retaining an excessively large amount of profits, thereby keeping stockholder relations more harmonious; (3) to the extent that profit diversion is linked to the amount of true profits (as assumed by Jones-Lee, Crew, and Rowley [27]) then the higher the true profits, the more profit diversion goes on. There appear to be other explanations why a firm may not want to report high profit. For instance, the firm may not want to engender union demands for a larger share of the pie, or the firm may not want to attract the attention of antitrust enforcers, since high profits may be viewed as a sign of excessive market power. As a result of this downward bias it may be more difficult to observe significant differences in profitability based on the control condition.

Three additional points concerning these studies are also worth noting. All of the studies examine average profitability even though, as Dennis Mueller notes [95, p. 210], marginal profitability is a more relevant term in viewing efficiency. It is possible for firms to have different average profits and yet, at the margin, to be equally profitable. Of course, firms provide information only on average profits. More important, none of the control studies distinguish between owners who are managers and owners not part of management. If the owner is the manager he has access to the same flow of other-than-profit sources of utility as the hired manager. If the owner is not part of the management he faces a very different set of incentives. Since he is not a manager he has only limited access to other-than-profit sources of utility and is not paid as a manager for any control activity. These distinctions will be developed in the following chapter. The profit studies also examined only one component of the stockholders return, a measure of his average rate of return. Stockholders are interested not only in rate of return but in the risk associated with this level of return as well. Boudreaux's is the only study to look at the variability of profits when examining profit rates. His and other studies viewing risk and the type of control will be examined next. Finally, these studies look at profit rates but neglect a treatment of what fraction of profits will be turned over to the stockholders as dividends. Stockholders are interested not only in the level of profits but the fraction of profits paid out in dividends.

Risk and Control Type

There has been recent interest in testing theories of "managerial enterprise" which predict that because of asymmetry in manager's reward structure, managers in the large corporation are less likely to take risks than owners.[q] It is argued that if a gamble is successful the hired manager is not likely to receive much of an increase in income but if the gamble fails, the manager faces possible dismissal. Moreover, stockholders' remoteness from the day-to-day activities of the firm makes it difficult for them to judge whether or not the manager maximizes profits. Consequently, the manager, rather than maximize profits, aims at achieving a gradual and steady appreciation in the firm's share price.

More recently, researchers have attempted to test hypotheses concerning differences between the manager's and owner's attitudes toward risk [17; 69; 101]. The procedure has been to select a sample of large firms, sort these firms into two categories, owner-controlled and manager-controlled, and then test for differences in risk between the two groups. The results of these studies have been mixed. One study found owner-controlled firms significantly more risky [17, p. 369], another found the *opposite* to be true—the manager-controlled group was significantly more risky [101, p. 230], and a third was inconclusive [69, p. 31]. Boudreaux relied on Baumol's comments concerning the asymmetry of the manager's payoff structure to examine the relationship between risk and the control type [17]. He used the standard deviation of profit rate as a measure of risk aversion. His sample consisted of the 36 owner-controlled and 36 manager-controlled firms, about 90 percent of which also appeared in the Monsen, Chiu, and Cooley sample [90]. The risk term was his dependent variable with control and industry dummies and their interaction terms as

---

[q] Although Baumol [9, p. 103] and Monsen and Downs [92] are most often cited as the authors of this view, the hired manager's aversion to risk was discussed over twenty years earlier. For example, Gordon in *Business Leadership in the Large Corporation* argued: "Among some professional executives, scientific caution may degenerate into a tendency to play safe. They do not receive the profits which may result from taking a chance, while their position in the firm may be jeopardized in the event of serious loss" [48, p. 324]. Beard noted that the hired manager, "forced to consider the stockholder or at least manage them" was placed in a position "conducive to anything but 'initiative' and 'leadership'." As a result "caution became his watchword; he shunned public discussion, and risky new enterprises" [11, p. 727].

his explanatory variables [17, p. 368]. He applied analysis of variance and found that owner-controlled firms were significantly more risky at the 0.01 level. The average standard deviation for the manager-controlled group was 3.07 percent, and the average of the owner-controlled group is 4.58 percent. Boudreaux concluded: ". . . the empirical finding that owner-controlled returns are more variable than manager-controlled is new, but is consistent with the arguments offered by the managerialists" [17, p. 370]. Boudreaux's results should be viewed with some reservation, however, in view of his sampling procedure.[r]

A second study by John Palmer noted at the outset that managers in manager-controlled firms have less to fear because of the control activity of stockholders than do managers in owner-controlled firms [101, p. 229]. He therefore argued that it is the managers in owner-controlled firms who are more reluctant to report exceptionally good or bad earnings, because these managers are less insulated from stockholder control [101, p. 228]. Palmer's hypothesis then was that managers in owner-controlled firms were less prone to risk taking than their counterparts in manager-controlled firms. Rather than use the standard deviation of profit rates, he used the coefficient of variation (standard deviation divided by average profit rate) from 1961 to 1969 as his dependent variable. He chose this because "it was felt that a large variance in the rate of return would be more acceptable to stockholders of firms also earning a high average rate of return . . ." [101, p. 229]. His sample consisted of the 500 top industrial corporations in 1965, which he divided into four size categories in increments of 125. His results indicated that only among the smallest size class was the difference in control groups significant, with the management-controlled firms displaying more variability in profits [101, p. 230]. He concluded that larger firms regardless of the control condition are more diverse and more insulated from the vagaries of the market place. Palmer later showed that his results

---

[r] Recall from the earlier discussion that Boudreaux's sample included the same twelve industries, the same time interval, and 64 of the 72 firms as in the Monsen, Chiu, and Cooley study. By comparing Boudreaux's published appendix [17, pp. 370-72] with an unpublished appendix [91] to the Monsen et al. study, differences between the two samples can be examined. One noticeable difference between the two samples is worth noting. Among manager-controlled firms in the motor vehicle industry, Boudreaux's sample included Fruehauf Corporation and International Harvester, while the Monsen et al. sample included Studebaker and American Motors. An examination of the profitability of these four firms during the period indicates that Studebaker and American Motors were extremely erratic from year to year, going from years of heavy losses to rates of return exceeding 30 percent. In contrast, Fruehauf and International Harvester displayed little variability. The standard deviations for all four firms were computed and Studebaker and American Motors were substituted for Fruehauf and International Harvester in the Boudreaux sample. While the average standard deviation for the entire manager-controlled group in Boudreaux's original sample was 3.07 percent, with the sample including Studebaker and American Motors it was 6.41 percent, more than twice Boudreaux's figure. This is larger than the owner-controlled average standard deviation of 4.58 percent. Thus, if Boudreaux's sample were generated by making substitutions in the Monsen et al. sample, as it appears, then these substitutions may have substantially affected his results.

were the same when he used simply the standard deviation of profits as his measure of risk [102, p. 128]. He also argued that the reason his results were at variance with those of Boudreaux was because Boudreaux failed to account fully for the effect of size on risk [102, p. 129].

Larner computed the variance of profits for 179 companies between 1956 and 1962 [69] and regressed this variance on control, size, and leverage variables, plus variables intended to account for the industry supply and demand conditions. He noted that the Baumol-Monsen and Downs hypothesis predicted a negative coefficient for the manager-controlled dummy variable, but he found a positive coefficient although it was not significant [69, p. 31]. His leverage term result was as expected, suggesting that firms with greater debt-asset ratios experienced greater variability in their return. Although the three studies are not strictly comparable, Larner's results fall somewhere between the other two studies. His use of a leverage term as an explanatory variable can be criticized because leverage is in part a policy variable; managers select a degree of leverage based on their risk aversion. To say that risk may differ between control types, then, is to say also that variables like leverage may differ between control types, and to the extent that leverage and control type are related, multicollinearity will result from using them both as explanatory variables.

Larner ignored any treatment of profit levels in analyzing risk. Boudreaux noted that owner-controlled firms were both more profitable and more risky but left it with that.[5] Palmer attempted to integrate both risk and return with his coefficient of variation, but in doing so he implicitly made an exact trade-off between risk and return that may or may not be the trade-off actually reflected in the market. It seems reasonable to assume that investors are more willing to tolerate larger standard deviations as long as higher profits are forthcoming, but it is another matter to assume that the coefficient of variation reflects precisely this trade-off.

A major problem once again with all three studies is that they coupled under the heading of owner-controlled firms both owner-managed firms and firms in which the owner is not part of management. An owner-manager aware of the day-to-day operations of the firm may view risk differently from the outside owner not in touch with the firm's operation. Monsen and Downs noted that it is the owners' remoteness from the day-to-day operation that makes the manager try to keep them happy by smoothing the profit stream. Palmer followed on this contention pointing out that it is the managers in the owner-controlled firms who most want to please stockholders since they can be replaced so easily if they do not. But he then proceeded to combine owner-managed firms with firms having an

---

[5] R.S. Bower, in a comment on Boudreaux, shows that for the period in question the manager-controlled firms may actually have done a better job for stockholders than owner-controlled firms when risk and return are considered [18].

outside owner. Certainly managers who are also controlling stockholders have more job security than the other managers.

Finally, in talking about the stockholders' attitudes toward risk, it would appear to matter whether we are talking about the average portfolio-balancing stockholder, who owns a modest share in many firms or a controlling stockholder, who, for whatever reason, has a large fraction of his wealth tied up in one firm. In all of the risk-based-on-type-of-control literature, stockholders have been viewed merely as a homogeneous group.

Retained Earnings and Control Type

Another implication of the alternative theories is that professional managers have a preference for retained earnings because these funds represent a source of discretion [139, p. 135], and provide a basis for growth [9; 83]. Three studies have attempted empirically to determine whether the type of control affects the retention policy of the firm [58; 126; 139]; and the results of the studies appear to conflict. O.E. Williamson, using the fraction of managers on the board of directors as a proxy for degree of management control, found that firms with higher internal representation on the board retained a significantly higher proportion of earnings [139, p. 136]. Kamerschen and Sorenson found the opposite to be true [58, p. 71; 126, p. 147].

Williamson's sample consisted of two firms in each of 26 industries. Using a paired-comparison technique, he compared the composition of the board and the retention ratio for the two firms in each industry for three annual observation periods [139, p. 136]. He concluded that firms with higher internal representation retain a significantly higher fraction of earnings [139, p. 137]. Again, as noted above in relation to compensation, Williamson's proxy depicts the type of control only as long as there is no correlation between internal representation and the actual control type based on the distribution of shares [139, p. 132]. This relationship will be examined in the next chapter.

Kamerschen selected the 140 industrials from his sample of 200 nonfinancial corporations and, using Larner's definition of control condition, concluded that the payout ratio from 1959 to 1964 was significantly higher (at the 0.01 level) in manager-controlled firms [58, p. 72]. Sorenson examined the firm's payout ratio over the period 1948-1966 for 30 owner-controlled and 30 manager-controlled firms drawn from a total of 11 industries [126]. After running an analysis of covariance for each industry with the payout ratio as the dependent variables he concluded: ". . . management-controlled firms had higher dividend payout ratios than owner-controlled firms . . . however, the differences were not statistically significant" [126, p. 147]. But he examined only differences within the individual industries and never tested for differences over his entire sample once the inter-industry differences were accounted for.

Sorenson's study provides the mean values of the payout ratios based on control type for each industry. Based on these data we ran an additional test using the Wilcoxon signed rank test for the paired observations for each industry. The results indicate that the manager-controlled group had a higher payout ratio and the difference between the two control groups was significant at the 0.02 level using a two-tailed test.

Of course, the relevant question is not how retention ratios differ across control types, since different firms have different investment opportunities, but how far the retention ratio differs from an optimal policy for that firm. Williamson and Sorenson at least attempted to adjust for differences in investment opportunities across industries by comparing firms in the same industry, but Kamerschen made no such adjustment. (Although in one sample he adjusts for leverage and finds the control variable remains significant [58, p. 72].) Kamerschen's and Sorenson's analyses also lump together, under the owner-controlled heading, firms that are owner-managed with firms controlled from the outside. But the owner-manager has access to the discretionary aspects of retained earnings whereas the outside owner does not. Finally O.E. Williamson's findings hinge on the acceptability of using the internal composition of the board of directors as a proxy for the degree of management control.

Summary of the Empirical Work

At the beginning of the century executive income consisted primarily of a salary that was relatively unresponsive to year-to-year fluctuations in performance. The bonus form of compensation became popular in the 1920s; it was little used during the depression but it is widely used again today. Various forms of contingent and deferred compensation also became more popular in the last few decades. The basic question remains whether the non-salary forms of compensation serve as incentive devices or are simply ways of paying managers which reduce the amount going in taxes. Gordon noted that during the 1930s, the bonus was an addition to salary rather than a substitute for it, but he felt that the bonus systems were not effective incentives. During the 1960s, the base salary of bonus recipients was lower than the base salary of nonbonus recipients in firms of equal size, suggesting that the bonus was in part a substitute for salary [25]. Roberts found that the form of compensation did not appear to affect the firm's profitability [109, p. 93]. Although the fraction of the firm held by top management has declined steadily since the 1904-1914 period, the value of a manager's holdings has remained large, and equity sources of income have become more important in terms of the manager's total income, particularly since the 1950 legislation conveying favorable tax treatment to stock options.

The early econometric work considering the relationship between compensation, profitability and firm sales found that manager's salary-plus-bonus was positively and significantly related to firm sales, but unrelated to profits. More recent research employing a more complete definition of income and adjusting for statistical problems encountered in the earlier studies has found executive incomes to be positively and significantly related to profits and the firm's market value, but unrelated to sales. The two studies that attempted to look at differences in compensation based on the type of control were inconclusive, but problems were noted concerning the definition of control and the statistical procedures employed. The literature concerning the incentives for promotion looked primarily at inter-firm executive mobility. There did not appear to be much mobility among top executives, possibly suggesting that there was little inter-firm competition for promotion. Little could be said about the criteria applied to intra-firm competition for promotion.

Trends in the ownership of large corporations indicate that individual dominant stockholders are becoming rare. Most studies concluded that effective control had passed increasingly to management, but a few studies noted the increasing dominance of the large financial institutions. Whether these institutions can exercise the control over management that was exercised by the dominant stockholder remains an unresolved issue. Thus far these institutions have shown little initiative in exercising control. The empirical work concerning the market for corporate control suggests that such a market exists, but there is some question concerning its sensitivity or its overall impact in disciplining the manager. There were also problems found in testing for the sensitivity of this market since the more finely tuned it is, the more difficult it becomes to observe differences between the firms that had been taken over and firms that had not.

The studies examining differences in profitability based on the type of control found, with some consistency, that owner-controlled firms had higher average profit rates than manager-controlled firms, but there was some question concerning the conclusions that could be drawn from this finding. The literature viewing differences in risk and differences in the retention policy based on control type yielded mixed results. All of the type of control studies coupled under the heading of owner-controlled those firms in which the owner was the manager with those firms in which the owner was not part of management even though these two owners face different incentives and constraints.

Overall there appears to be a basic inconsistency in the empirical results. On the one hand it was shown that the manager's compensation structure encourages him to act in the stockholders' interests, but on the other hand the owner-controlled firms appear to be more profitable than manager-controlled firms. Should one, therefore, conclude that these differences in profitability are due to some factor other than differences in pay incentives? This question will be examined in the following chapter.

4 Management Incentives and Constraints Under Three Different Control Conditions

Introduction

The extensive empirical work on the consequences of control condition still leaves many questions unsettled. The examination of differences in firm risk based on owner or management control showed that manager-controlled firms were significantly more risky [101] or significantly less risky [17], depending on whose results were examined. Likewise, the examination of retained earnings revealed manager-controlled firms either retained significantly more earnings [139] or significantly less [58; 126] earnings, depending on the study. Two findings which appeared with more uniformity were that managers were paid to produce profit and market value, and that firms with a dominant stockholding interest appeared to have higher rates of return than manager-controlled firms. But even these findings, taken together, are somewhat inconsistent—on the one hand the findings suggest that managers are paid to perform in the stockholders' interests while on the other hand there actually is a difference in performance based on control type. When the dominant stockholder is also the manager it is clear that he faces a different incentive structure from other managers, but when a dominant stockholder hires a manager does the hired manager's compensation structure differ from the structure facing managers in manager-controlled firms? By failing to examine that question, the previous empirical work would have us believe that managers have similar compensation structures regardless of control type; why, then, is there a difference in performance?

There has not yet been a satisfactory examination of managers' compensation structures based on type of control. The two studies that looked at the question both have serious limitations. O.E. Williamson examined the level of compensation between two control types, manager and owner, but lacking data on the actual control situation he relied on the proportion of managers on the board of directors as his proxy for management control [139]. It will be shown that such a proxy is misleading, for firms with a dominant stockholder appear to have a significantly higher proportion of managers on the board of directors than do firms without a dominant stockholder. Therefore when Williamson used the proportion of managers on the board as his measure of the degree of management control, he more likely was observing the degree of owner control.

Robert Larner also attempted to examine firms based only on two control situations [69], so he combined under the heading of "owner-controlled" those firms with a dominant outside stockholder and those firms with a dominant stockholder as manager, even though the managers are likely to face different incentives and constraints. Nearly all of the previous studies which examined performance characteristics such as profitability, risk, or retention based on the type of control have sorted firms into only two categories: (1) owner-controlled firms, consisting of all firms with a dominant stockholder, whether outsider or manager; and (2) manager-controlled firms. It will be shown here that attempting to test hypotheses concerning the theory of the firm based on this twofold classification has led to ambiguous and inconsistent results. If firms are to be sorted at all, a more useful way of sorting them is with a three-part classification system: (1) firms with a dominant stockholder but a hired manager, (2) firms with a dominant stockholder who also serves as manager, and (3) firms without a dominant stockholder. This classification system follows logically when one focuses on conditions affecting incentives and constraints facing an individual manager, and using it also clears up the ambiguity found in earlier empirical research.

In this chapter several hypotheses will be developed and tested concerning the compensation structures of firms that are of the three different control types, and the effects of control type on the performance of firms will be examined in the following chapter. The next section will be devoted to uncovering the effects of control type on the incentives and constraints facing the manager. Implications will be drawn from previous analysis on the theory of the firm, particularly the work of Williamson [139], Marris [83], Baumol [9], Monsen and Downs [90], Galbraith [43; 44], and Gordon [48]. A theoretical framework will then be developed to examine compensation structures under three control conditions, and hypotheses concerning differences in the compensation structures under each control condition will be developed. These hypotheses will then be tested in the third section using a sample of 48 firms drawn from three industries. Another aspect of the incentives and constraints facing the manager, job tenure, will be examined under the three control conditions in the fourth. The final section will summarize the principal findings and state the main conclusions.

Incentives and Constraints Based on Control Type

The number of elements that conceivably could enter a manager's utility function seems endless, for it would include all forms of payment to the manager whether they consist of income, leisure, the prestige associated with firm size, the working environment, the extent of surveillance by stockholders, or what have you. In addition to income, the single element most often cited by the alternative theories of the firm is firm size [9; 44; 48; 83; 90; 139]. Assume the manager's utility is a function of his income, I, firm size, S, and n other forms of nonpecuniary benefits, N_i. Thus,

$$U = U(I, S, N_i) \qquad i = 1, 2, \ldots n.$$

In stating the manager's utility function, nothing yet is being said about his opportunity set. An important point here is that the manager views consumption of nonpecuniary benefits as inferior to an equivalent increase in money income since money usually offers a wider range of choice [42, p. 1152]. Hence the manager will always prefer a dollar (after taxes) to an additional dollar devoted to additional size or nonpecuniary benefits.

All of the alternative theories require the manager to meet some minimum performance constraint measured in terms of profits [9; 44; 139] or the firm's market value [83], to keep stockholders satisfied. If his performance drops below a specified level, some of the stockholders will grow dissatisfied with the manager and sell their holdings. This selling can cause the price of the share to drop to a point where the firm becomes an attractive target for a takeover. Thus, the minimum profit constraint is determined by the transaction costs involved in reforming or replacing the manager. These transaction costs consist of the cost of (1) detecting the diversion of profits, (2) acquiring the control necessary to reform or replace the manager, and, finally, (3) policing this profit diversion.

Part of the transaction costs of control is the cost of detecting profit diversion. If a potential reformer has specific information about the firm's potential profitability then he need only consider the firm's reported profits to get some idea about profit diversion. But information about the firm's potential profitability is not easily acquired, and the potential reformer may need to observe specific instances of profit diversion to know that such diversion is going on. It is here that the transaction costs of detection may depend upon the form that profit diversion takes. For example, if the manager chooses to divert one million dollars in profits and take it as a higher salary, this would be more easily observable than if the same manager decides to allow profits to slip by the same amount as a result of on-the-job leisure. If a dollar diverted to two forms of nonpecuniary benefits yields equal satisfaction to the manager, then one might expect the manager to choose the form that is least detectable.

Of course, simply positing a minimum profit constraint begs the question of how much discretion the manager really has. The relevant question is how close is this minimum to the firm's potential profitability under a profit-maximizing manager. If the transaction costs of replacing the manager are trivially small then the minimum profit constraint will be close to the firm's potential. And the manager's preference for sales or other nonpecuniary benefits will then present no serious threat to the stockholders' investment because if the manager can be replaced so easily he will simply be paid the "going wage" determined in the market for executives, and he will be quickly reformed or replaced if he attempts to divert profits to his own ends. But as the transaction costs involved in removing the manager grow large, the manager's range of discretion grows as well.

One of the less obvious transaction costs of control is the cost of acquiring the degree of control that is necessary to reform or replace the management. This may involve the outright purchase of a controlling number of shares, the solicitation of a sufficient number of proxy votes, or the acquisition of the firm through merger. Henry Manne has discussed these aspects of the cost of control at length [79; 80; 82], and they will not be discussed here. Finally, the actual policing of the management must be considered. These policing costs may include what O.E. Williamson terms the "transition costs" of replacing an incumbent manager [140]. Although Williamson feels these costs are difficult to quantify, he notes that they can be substantial [140, p. 316]. Marris also notes the high cost of replacing management and argues that even when control is in the hands of a few stockholders, transition costs provide some insulation from management, since a new manager will not be familiar with the daily workings of the particular firm even if he is from the same industry. Marris therefore concludes that "even in a fairly closely-held company, the management has considerable autonomy . . ." [83, p. 17].

In order to avoid later confusion, let us provide a brief description of the control-condition terminology that is to be used in this study and is thought to reflect the crucial determinants of constraints facing managers. The basic difference between the twofold definitions of control condition used in previous analyses and the threefold definitions to be used in this study is that firms with a dominant stockholder which had previously been defined as owner-controlled will be split here into two categories, firms in which the dominant stockholder is also the manager (owner-managed firms) and firms in which the dominant stockholder is not part of management (externally-controlled firms). The definition of the manager-controlled group remains the same as before and simply denotes the absence of any dominant stockholder. Table 4-1 summarizes the terminology and abbreviations to be used in this study and compares our definitions with those previously employed.

Thus far only the manager's utility function plus some bounds on the range of his discretion have been discussed, but now by distinguishing control conditions we pursue the remaining question: How does the manager's opportunity set differ under each type of control? The manager's incentive structure under a dominant outside stockholder will be examined

**Table 4-1
Definitions of Control**

Previous Definitions	Control	Management	Revised Definitions
Owner-Controlled	= Owner	Owner	= Owner-Managed (OM)
Owner-Controlled	= Owner	Manager	= Externally-Controlled (EC)
Manager-Controlled	= Manager	Manager	= Manager-Controlled (MC)

first, followed by the incentive structure in manager-controlled firms where no dominant stockholding interest prevails. Finally, the incentive structure in an owner-managed firm will be discussed. The three types of control will be compared and testable implications will be noted.

Managerial Incentives in Externally-Controlled (EC) Firms

Assume there is a dominant stockholder who is not part of management but possesses enough votes to control the manager. Since he is not part of management, the dominant stockholder does not have access to the non-pecuniary benefits which interest the manager, and, consequently, he is interested only in the return on his investment. Faced with a manager having the utility function described earlier, how should the dominant stockholder ensure a maximum return on his investment? If the cost of replacing the manager is zero, then the owner can simply pay him the market wage for executives, and fire him if he tries to divert profits to his own ends. But if the transaction costs involved in replacing the manager are non-trivial then the owner will not fire the manager unless the owner's share of the expected gains resulting from a change in managers will exceed the cost of replacing him.[a] If the owner is aware of the firm's potential value then he need refer only to its market value to determine the extent of profit diversion by the manager. But if the owner is not sure of the firm's potential, he may have to rely on specific observations of profit diversion for this information. So the owner's ability to detect diversion may depend on the form of this diversion.

---

[a] A simple way of viewing this is as follows: Allow m to equal the fraction of the firm owned by the dominant stockholder, V^* to be equal to the potential market value of the firm if the manager is replaced, V to be the market value of the firm with the existing level of profit diversion, and T to be the transaction costs of replacing the manager. The manager will be replaced if

$$m(V^* - V) > T.$$

Control conveys not only the ability to hire and fire, but also the power to structure the manager's pay package. Faced with some amount of profit diversion short of the magnitude required to warrant firing the manager, the owner can structure the manager's income scheme so he is penalized for profit diversion. If the manager wants to divert profits, then the compensation package designed to maximize the firm's present value should take into account both pecuniary and nonpecuniary forms of compensation. Masson discusses an optimal compensation package, arguing that the compensation scheme designed to maximize the present value of the firm should penalize the manager for pushing sales beyond the point which maximizes present value. And if compensation does not fall, *ceteris paribus*, past this point then either the compensation scheme is not structured to maximize present value or the manager does not derive satisfaction from increased sales [86, p. 1282].

Such a residual compensation scheme is attractive to the owner for a couple reasons. By linking the manager's marginal compensation to his performance, the owner need not be as concerned with the form that profit diversion takes; whether the manager pursues the "quiet life," more attractive surroundings, or whatever, these diversions will cost the manager something in foregone income; and indeed the more difficult these diversions are to track down, the more attractive the residual compensation structure becomes. Some support for this methodological approach can be drawn from Furubotn and Pejovich, who note in their discussion of alternative firm goals that "By conceiving of the basic problem as one involving tradeoff relations, it is possible to use conventional theory to infer the behavior of the corporation regardless of what the goals are" [42, p. 1150].

The more the manager is penalized for marginal decreases in profits, *ceteris paribus*, the more costly diversion of profits becomes. For a given level of managerial utility, the optimal compensation structure is one designed so that the cost to the manager of diverting one more dollar to his own ends is equal to the cost to the stockholders in foregone profits as a result of surrendering that dollar. By expanding part of the basic model developed by Williamson [139], the point can be shown using a simple utility function consisting of income and "staff."[b] Figure 4-1 gives a simplified geometrical presentation of the basic proposition. Along the vertical axis is measured both profit and the manager's income, and along the horizontal axis is measured expenses on staff. Curve AA shows the maximum gross profit obtainable by the firm at each level of staff. U_0 is the manager's indifference curve between income and staff (and all the *nonpecuniary* benefits that go with staff). Assume that U_0 represents the

---

[b] Note that this definition of staff is revised somewhat from Williamson's original formulation to include only nonpecuniary expenditures. The external controller structures compensation so that the manager is not paid for staff, *ceteris paribus*, as is assumed in Williamson's formulation.

Figure 4-1. Manager's Income-Staff Trade-off

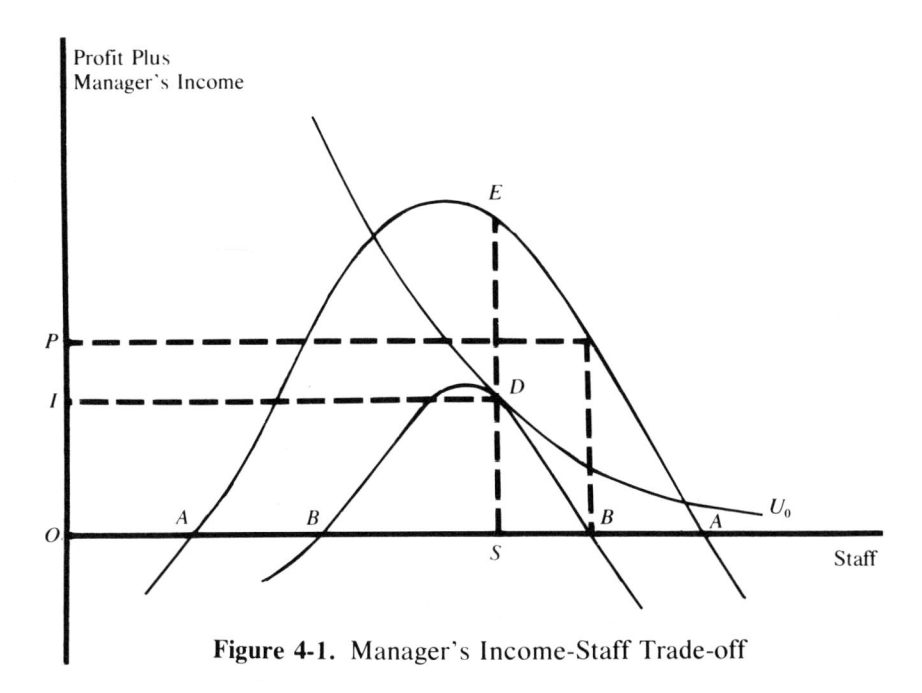

minimum level of utility that will keep the manager from changing jobs. Given U_0 and AA, what incentive scheme maximizes profit net of payment to the manager? The optimal compensation is one designed so that the cost to the manager of one more dollar of "staff" equals the cost to the stockholders of foregoing that dollar. Thus the optimal structure in this model is a residual compensation system that turns over to the manager all profits above OP. This confronts the manager with an opportunity set represented by the curve BB, which has the same slope as points directly above it on AA because it is merely the top part of curve AA, lowered to the horizontal axis. The manager maintains utility level U_0 at point D where he is consuming OI in income and OS in staff. This leaves $DE = OP$ in profits to the stockholders, which is the maximum vertical distance between AA and U_0. This model can be expanded to other nonpecuniary benefits as long as one maintains the assumption that the external-controller does not permit the manager to tie his income to these goals.

An additional advantage for the owner lies in the residual compensation structure over the fixed salary. The residual compensation scheme forces the manager to bear some of the risk associated with the firm's performance. To the extent that market forces or managerial behavior cause period-to-period fluctuations in profit or market value the manager whose income is tied to profits or market value is paid more in good times and less in bad times. Consequently the amount remaining for stockholders varies less than it would if the manager drew a fixed salary. To the extent that stockholders are risk averse they may prefer the smoother profit stream. And to the extent that managers are risk averse they may attempt to smooth the period-to-period fluctuations in profit or market value.

Manager Incentives in Manager-Controlled (MC) Firms

The major operational difference between EC firms and MC firms is that the transaction costs of replacing the manager are likely to be higher in the MC firm. Any potential reformer must first undergo the cost of acquiring control of an MC firm, but the external-controller already possesses this power by definition. Since the transaction costs of control are higher in the MC firms, we can expect their managers to have a wider range of discretion, and it is natural to expect them to use some of this discretion in structuring the form of their compensation package. How might one expect their compensation packages to differ from an incentive structure explicitly designed to maximize profits? The alternative theories were discussed in Chapter 2 and need not be reviewed here, but each has a lot to say about the managers' compensation packages. Moreover, these views were explicitly formulated for an environment where there is a separation of ownership from control.

Marris [83, p. 64], Baumol [9, p. 46], Williamson [139, p. 34], and Galbraith [43, p.101; 44, p. 116] all rely heavily on the empirical claim that the manager's income is very much related to firm size, but has little to do with stockholder related variables such as profitability. And one need not rely only on recent literature to find references concerning the link between salary and size. N.S. Buchanan discussed this relationship over thirty-five years ago [20, p. 82]. In fact, in the earlier part of this century this preoccupation with size seemed even more prevalent. Some firms, like Singer Sewing Machine, Inc., for example, didn't even report the firm's annual profit in the 1920s. They simply reported assets [39; 1973, p. 167].

To the extent that the manager is paid his marginal product, and to the extent that increases in staff and assets will raise this marginal product, then the pursuit of size appears to be a rational way for the manager to raise his income. But the alternative theories take the link between salary and size beyond this. Statements like "even if size did not promote profits" [9, p. 46] or salaries "do not vary with profits" [44, p. 116] indicate the view that profits have little impact on salary.[c]

As noted earlier, the more the manager's income is linked to profits or to market value, the more costly to him profit diversion becomes and the more

---
[c] In Chapter 2 we noted that some of the alternative theories concede incentive value to compensation schemes other than salary. Baumol [10, p. 81] and Marris [83, p. 77] both see a limited role for stock options in creating profit incentives, but Williamson [135, pp. 300-306] and Galbraith [44, p. 116] see less of a role for various incentive schemes.

variable his income stream will be. Size is a more attractive item for a manager to tie his salary to, for along with size comes a host of nonpecuniary benefits including increased security.[d] An income stream tied to firm size is also likely to vary much less than one tied to profits or market value, since size varies much less from year to year.

Does all this mean that the managers in MC firms are "better off" than managers in EC firms? Not necessarily. Although the alternative theories would have us believe that they are, since the manager in the absence of stockholder control can pursue firm size plus all the pecuniary and nonpecuniary goods that go with size, Alchian argues that competition for jobs among executives ensures that any net advantages of one job over another will be competed away. The managers in manager-controlled firms may receive a different form or different mix of income, but the total package is not necessarily more attractive: "Instead they are getting paid with a different, higher cost (i.e., less efficient), vector of rewards—one that costs more to provide but is no more preferable on net than those used in other corporations" [1, p. 345]. This vector of compensation is different because the costs of initiating control to restructure the compensation package, "say one with higher wages and less leisure," exceed the expected gains to be made as a result of this restructuring [1, p. 346].

Although the evidence on executive mobility does not indicate as active a market for executives as Alchian's remarks suggest, there should be a long-run tendency for firms of each control type to offer comparable levels of compensation. Otherwise each control type would be unable to attract executives of comparable ability; and there is no evidence that the managers in EC firms are less qualified.[e] Thus if the "extent of surveillance" [1, p. 346] by a dominant stockholder conveys disutility to the manager and there are no offsetting nonpecuniary advantages in these firms,[f] then,

[d] Although all the alternative theories mentioned equate size of firm with security, none is very explicit as to why this should be. Marris simply notes that "a large firm is more difficult to take over than a small firm" and "a large firm in a crisis is more easily able to find temporary assistance than a small firm" [83, p. 68]. But as Marris points out, if the firm pursues size too vigorously, retains too large a fraction of earnings, is levered too highly, or continues to invest in relatively unprofitable endeavors, then its market value may drop to the point where an outsider will find the firm an attractive target for a raid. Nevertheless, Marris indicates that the manager has a very large range of discretion. He makes some "numerical calculations based on statistical observations" and concludes that a firm pursuing size can allow the stock market value to drop by one-third over what it would be if the market value were maximized, and "the growth oriented management could safely continue the policy indefinitely, even if there were quite a number of others who chose to behave otherwise" [84, p. 44].

[e] Competition between firms for the top executives may not be obvious, but if firms expect to compete on equal footing for fresh MBA's, then the career prospects in each firm must be equally attractive.

[f] There is some evidence in the popular business literature that managers do not prefer to work in firms with dominant stockholders because management in these firms tends to be more tightly controlled. A series done by the *Wall Street Journal* in early 1975 entitled, "The Scions" indicates that positions in family firms are viewed as less attractive by professional managers.

ceteris paribus, externally-controlled firms should receive a higher level of money wages than manager-controlled firms. Although the cost of the vector of compensation may be higher in manager-controlled firms, these managers are not necessarily better off because a dollar in income is preferred to a dollar's worth of nonpecuniary benefits.

Thus the comparison of the compensation structure in EC firms with that in MC firms is really a comparison of a structure designed to maximize profits with a structure more in harmony with managers' interests, as discussed by the alternative theories of the firm. Two testable sets of implications can be drawn from all of this. First, EC managers will be paid more at the margin for profits and market value, and less for sales, *ceteris paribus*, than managers in MC firms. Second, to the extent that advantages of employment in MC firms are valued by executives and are competed away in the form of lower wages by competition among executives, then MC firms will exhibit a lower level of wages than EC firms.

The Owner-Manager's (OM) Incentives

The owner-manager by definition has a large stake in the firm, but he also has a wider margin for discretion than either of the other managers. Although profit diversion becomes more costly as the owner-manager's holdings in the firm increase, none has denied that he might pander to his own special nonpecuniary tastes. J.A. Schumpeter recognized the first drive of an entrepreneur as "the dream and the will to found a kingdom" [113, p. 93]. Frank Knight also emphasized "the impulse to create," noting "the desire for increased income is not the dominant motive in much of this" [64, p. 162]. R.A. Gordon compared the motives of professional managers with those of owner-managers and pointed out that the tendency "to continue to expand in the face of declining profits" may be no stronger among hired managers than among owner-entrepreneurs [48, pp. 331-32].

The federal income tax structure also can make profit diversion attractive even for a sole owner, and it is increasingly attractive as the ownership interest is lower. For example, assume that all profits are paid out as dividends and the sole owner's personal income tax bracket is 50 percent. Then after both corporate income taxes (50 percent) and personal income taxes are applied, a dollar's worth of nonpecuniary benefits costs him only twenty-five cents in foregone dividends. Furthermore, if the dominant stockholder owns only 20 percent of the firm, he pays only five cents on the dollar for nonpecuniary benefits. Hence, despite his sizable ownership interest the owner-manager can still have an incentive to behave as a "free rider" and divert profits to his own ends at the expense of other taxpayers and other stockholders.

It seems more difficult to predict on an a priori basis what form his compensation will take since he may claim income both as managerial compensation and as his share of residual profits. But since executive compensation represents a cost to the firm and is netted out before the corporate income tax is applied, it may be more attractive in after-tax terms for the owner-manager to take his income as managerial compensation rather than as his share of dividends or capital gains. A dollar in dividends or capital gains is taxed twice—both under corporate taxes and as personal income or capital gains.[g] Of course the Internal Revenue Service may not view an exorbitant salary favorably.

The point is that simply because the manager owns a sizable fraction of the firm he may not lose interest in taking some of his income in kind, or in diverting it to a higher salary. The current tax laws make this behavior more attractive. So past empirical work, which combined EC and OM firms under owner-controlled firms in viewing compensation, could have been combining two quite different and distinct groups. And there is another, institutional, reason for viewing the OM firms as a distinct group. Based on the 1964 revision of the Qualified Stock Options Section of the Internal Revenue Code, any manager owning 5 percent or more of the firm is not eligible for stock options [70, p. 317]. According to Lewellen's sample of 50 top corporations, stock options represented, on average, about one-third of the manager's after-tax income (excluding ownership income) between 1964 and 1969 [71, p. 119]. With such a large source of income closed to owner-managers, it would seem unwise to combine owner-managed firms with externally-controlled firms in studies of compensation. Indeed, the different tax circumstances that are apt to separate owner-managed firms from manager-controlled firms because of differences in wealth of the managers will plague all comparisons that are attempting to uncover other effects.

Statistical Test of the Impact of Control Type on Compensation Structure

In this section a statistical model will be developed to test implications drawn from the previous section concerning the differences in compensation structure among control types. The data and statistical methodology will be described in the first part. The hypotheses to be tested and the regression results will be presented in the second part.

---

[g] In Appendix A a model is developed to examine the owner-manager's income under various fractions of ownership. The relationship of the chief executive's salary with salaries of other executives in the firm is also considered.

Data and Methodology

Nearly all of the discussion of the separation of ownership from control is in the context of the large industrial firm and we are concerned with such a population as well. Our sample will therefore consist of sixteen large firms from each of three SIC three-digit industries that possess large firms. The three industries selected were drugs, chemicals, and petroleum refining; firms were drawn from the Securities and Exchange Commission's *Directory of Companies* filing annual reports with the SEC in 1971 [115].[h] A primary requirement for firm selection was the availability of a complete series of proxy statements on file with the SEC. More than a dozen firms had incomplete files and could not be used.[i] The firms in the sample represent about 70 percent of all industry sales,[j] so even with some missing firms, the sample represents a sizable portion of each industry.

The objective was to select a time interval that was long enough to limit the influence of short-term irregularities, but short enough so that the management could be thought of as continuous over the period since changes in management often caused abrupt year-to-year fluctuations in compensation. The period selected was also constrained by the availability of information on file with the SEC. For years prior to 1969 the data became increasingly more spotty. For these reasons the time period selected was 1969 through 1972, and all variables are yearly averages over the period.

Dependent Variables. A single dependent variable, executive compensation, was used for this analysis.

---

[h] The number of industries selected was somewhat limited by the difficulty of gathering the data and the statistical procedure involved. The SEC imposes a daily limit on the number of files that can be requested. If this limit is exceeded the SEC imposes "overtime charges," a practice that seems inappropriate for a government agency whose explicit purpose is to make information available to the public. The information is not only difficult and costly to retrieve, in addition there are large, unexplained gaps in the files which make research in this area particularly troublesome.

[i] The sampling procedure employed was as follows. First, given the difficulty of compiling the data, the sample size was limited to sixteen firms in each of three industries, or 48 firms in all. Since all previous research on the diffusion of ownership indicated that firms with a dominant stockholder were greatly outnumbered by firms without a dominant stockholder, firms with a dominant stockholder were selected first to ensure adequate representation in the sample of this minority group. A total of 22 firms with complete sets of data (nearly all from the top 500 firms based on assets) were so chosen. Of course this dominant stockholder group was later divided into owner-managed and externally-controlled firms based on our definitions of control. The remainder of the sample, consisting of firms without a dominant stockholder, or manager-controlled firms, was drawn randomly (alphabetically) to round out each industry at 16 firms each (again, nearly all of these firms were from the top 500 based on assets). As it turned out, firms of each of the three control types were evenly distributed among the industries. The sample is listed in Appendix C.

[j] This was computed based on a listing of all firms in the industry as of 1967 [37].

Executive Compensation. The compensation of the *chief* executive of each firm was used as the measure of executive compensation. Focusing on only the chief executive may appear to restrict the relevance of the results, but every study to examine the relationship between the top executive's pay and that of other executive officers has found that pay is carefully scaled and therefore highly correlated among executive levels [25; 70; 119]. Hence the factors that influence the compensation of the top executive can be presumed to affect the other managerial pay levels as well.

Two measures of compensation were used: before-tax salary plus bonus and total after-tax compensation. The first definition was used for several reasons. Since it was used in all previous analysis of executive compensation, it was used here to allow comparability with these earlier studies. Also, to the extent that compensation serves as a conspicuous index of executive status and prestige, before-tax salary plus bonus is highly visible and may convey psychic value to the chief executive regardless of the after-tax value. Finally this measure is not subject to the unavoidably arbitrary tax and present value calculations involved in computing the fuller definition of compensation.

The more complete definition of compensation employed consists of after-tax compensation, including the present value of retirement benefits, deferred compensation, stock options, and contributions to savings plans. The proper treatment of deferred and contingent forms of compensation is a lengthy process involving discounting for both mortality and futurity. The approach used in this study is quite similar to that developed by Lewellen in his extensive study of executive compensation [70]. The current income equivalent of the various deferred and contingent forms of compensation was computed for each chief executive. This consisted of the amount of additional direct cash that would have been required to reward the manager as well after taxes as he was with the various forms of compensation he actually received. In the case of pension plans, for example, the procedure was to determine the additional compensation the executive would require to purchase from an insurance company an individual retirement annuity with an identical return as his pension.[k]

It should be noted that although stock options are included the dividends and capital gains that a manager receives from his *personal* holdings in the firm are not considered in this definition of after-tax compensation. After-tax compensation was kept separate from equity-related income to avoid the following identification problem. To the extent that a manager will buy into a more successful firm or choose not to purchase shares in a less successful one (and stock options make the decision quite easy), there is a natural link between the amount of equity-related income and perfor-

---

[k] A fuller explanation of all procedures employed can be found in Appendix B.

mance variables such as profit and market value. It will be shown later that the inclusion of equity-related income would have served only to reinforce the findings in this study. Another reason for not including equity-related income is that, strictly speaking, this income is not paid to the executive in his capacity as manager, but in his capacity as risk bearer.

In the absence of specific information concerning the exemptions and deductions that each executive actually reported, it was assumed that all executives claimed the standard deductions rather than itemized deductions. This assumption was made to preserve uniformity and comparability among the after-tax compensation figures, and of course because itemized individual returns are not available. Since the primary interest of this study is with relative rather than absolute levels of after-tax compensation, these simplifying assumptions should not cause serious distortions.[1]

All of the raw data for the compensation calculations were found in the firm's statement proxy or in the Form 10-K filed by the firm with the SEC.

Explanatory Variables. Four explanatory variables were used in this analysis: stockholder welfare, size, control type, and industry.

Stockholder Welfare Variable. Two measures of stockholder welfare were used: the level of the firm's accounting profit and its market value. The accounting profit has been the most commonly used index of stockholders' welfare in previous studies related to compensation. It will be employed here primarily to allow comparability with earlier analysis. But various accounting options, such as differing depreciation policies, can result in inconsistent reporting procedures across firms. The use of reported accounting profit as a measure of stockholder welfare also implies no conflict between short- and long-run profit maximization or no real trade-off between increasing the current year's net income and increasing the present value of the entire stream of income. Yet if a chief executive, nearing retirement, has his compensation tied to current profit, he may be tempted to cut back on any expenditures which would erode current profit even though they might increase the present value of the firm. Moreover, reported profits convey no information about the year-to-year variability of profits or the fraction of profits that are returned to stockholders as dividends. Two firms producing the same average profits may be valued differently if the variability of their profit streams differ. Also if one firm is paying out dividends at a rate more preferable to stockholders than the other, it may conceivably be valued more highly. As R.A. Gordon noted

---

[1]Of course if the deduction policy differed systematically across control types this could introduce problems. The discounting procedure employed in computing present values could also introduce a bias to the extent that the age of managers differs across control types. As a check on this the age composition of managers was examined and found not to be different between control types.

over thirty years ago: "The mere existence of profits on the company's books is not enough; some group must have a right to claim them" [48, p. 336].

All this suggests that short-run profitability may not be the most appropriate stockholder-welfare variable. The recent finance literature indicates that the maximization of the value of the firm may be a less ambiguous managerial goal [47; 118, Ch. 9]. To the extent that the firm's market value takes into account current and expected profits as well as risk and retention policy, it appears to be a better measure of overall performance than profits. And if the manager's income scheme is tied to the value of the firm, there is no trade-off between current and expected profits. Therefore, the firm's market value can be more appropriate as a performance measure, and it will also be used as an alternative measure of stockholder welfare.[m] The market value variable used is the year-end common market value of the firm taken from the annual *Fortune* list [40].

Size. The other explanatory variable used in all previous analysis is some measure of size. Previous research indicates that all the alternative measures of size, whether value added, assets, employment, or sales, are very close substitutes [83, p. 89]. Since Baumol's work is couched specifically in terms of sale, and since sales has been the most commonly used measure of size in previous research, sales will be used in this analysis. The sales term is taken each year from the annual *Fortune* list [40].

Control Type. Any determination of the fraction of the firm required for control that is short of an absolute majority is inherently arbitrary. Over the years the fraction defined as required for working control has dropped from 20 percent with Berle and Means [15] to no specific percentage requirement in Burch's study [21]. The explanation usually given for this drop has been that the more dispersed the holdings become, the smaller is the fraction required for control. All previous research sorted firms into either firms with a dominant stockholder (owner-controlled) or firms without a dominant stockholder (manager-controlled). Some of the empirical work discussed in the previous chapter which examined the effects of the type of control on performance of firms used a very careful procedure in selecting firm based on control type, ruling out any firms which were not clearly owner-controlled or manager-controlled. Other studies sorted all firms into one category or another, and thereby proposed a stronger test since no firms were arbitrarily eliminated. This study will follow the latter procedure but will sort firms into three categories: (1) externally-controlled

---

[m] Of course the firm's market value is subject to a large number of random forces. To the extent that these forces affect one firm control type more than others there could be problems with this measure of performance.

firms, defined as firms with a dominant interest holding 4 percent or more of the common stock and is not part of the management; (2) manager-controlled firms, defined as having no single dominant interest owning 4 percent or more of the stock; and (3) owner-managed firms where the chief executive owns either directly or beneficially (immediate family) 4 percent or more of the stock.[n] The information on control type was drawn from the individual proxy statements and from the empirical work examining the extent of the separation of ownership and control [21; 23; 69; 104; 105].

Industry Variables. Since the sample was drawn from three different industries, dummy variables will be introduced to account for inter-industry differences. This adjustment appears necessary for several reasons. O.E. Williamson's examination of the level of salary indicated that salary was significantly related to barriers to entry and concentration even when profits were included as an additional explanatory variable [139, p. 133]. Roberts also found the industry to be important in determining the level of compensation [109, p. 33]. There was also evidence in the proxy statements that firms felt they were competing for executive talent with other firms in the same industry.[o] Another reason why industry factors should be considered is that the extent of market power in an industry may dictate how much discretion the managers have in devising their compensation structure. Of the three industries selected, the drug industry has been defined by Mann as having "very high" entry barriers and the chemical and petroleum industries both have "substantial" entry barriers [79].

Statistical Procedure. In the absence of any particular theoretical justification to specify the relationship otherwise, regression equations will be linear. The basic structural form of the relationship can be written as follows:

$$C_i = \alpha_0 + \alpha_1 P_i + \alpha_2 S_i + \mu_i \qquad (4.1)$$

where C_i represents executive compensation, P_i is reported profits, S_i is firm sales, and μ_i is the random disturbance term with mean zero and variance σ_μ^2. In the regression the coefficients α_1 and α_2 register the marginal impact that changes in profits and sales have on executive compensation, and each is a means of estimating the relative importance of one explanatory variable on compensation. Profits and sales will be used

---

[n] The percentage required for control is relatively low so as to insure an adequate representation among the dominant stockholder groups. In a few cases it was not clear from the proxy statement who the chief executive was; in those cases the list of chief executives provided in the *Forbes* annual survey was relied upon. One firm (Clark Oil Company) changed from an owner-managed to an externally-controlled firm in 1970 and was defined here as the latter.

[o] For example, one drug company explained a new bonus plan to its shareholder as follows: "Many of the company's pharmaceutical competitors have similar bonus plans and the board of directors believes the plan will help attract and retain key managerial personnel" [110].

primarily because they have been used in all previous research, but for reasons discussed earlier, the firm's market value will also be substituted for profits as in (4.2):

$$C_i = \beta_0 + \beta_1 V_i + \beta_2 S_i + \omega_i \qquad (4.2)$$

where V_i is the firm's market value, S_i is the firm sales and ω_i is the random disturbance term with mean zero and variance σ_ω^2.

Since the main objective of this analysis is to examine the differences in the compensation structure among control types, some additional terms will be introduced to account for the type of control. The easiest way to compare the coefficients of the three control groups is to include dummy variables to take into account not only differences in the level of compensation, but differences in the marginal impact that profits and sales have on compensation. The dummy variables to be introduced are as follows:

$$\text{OM} \begin{cases} = 1 \text{ if firm } i \text{ is owner-managed} \\ = 0 \text{ elsewhere} \end{cases}$$

$$\text{MC} \begin{cases} = 1 \text{ if firm } i \text{ is manager-controlled} \\ = 0 \text{ elsewhere} \end{cases}$$

When both OM and MC are zero the firm is externally-controlled (EC). Expression (4.3) includes the control dummy variables as both intercept and slope terms:[p]

$$C_i = \alpha_0 + \alpha_1 \text{OM} + \alpha_2 \text{MC} + \alpha_3 P_i + \alpha_4 \text{OM} P_i + \alpha_5 \text{MC} P_i \\ + \alpha_6 S_i + \alpha_7 \text{OM} S_i + \alpha_8 \text{MC} S_i + \mu_i. \qquad (4.3)$$

Differences in the level of compensation between the EC group and the OM group are estimated by α_1, and differences between the EC group and the MC group are estimated by α_2. Differences between the EC and OM groups in the marginal impact that profits and sales have on compensation are estimated by the coefficients α_4 and α_7, and between the EC and MC groups, by the coefficients α_5 and α_8. If there is no difference between the control types then these terms will not be significantly different from zero. But if, for example, the MC group pays their managers significantly more for sales (or penalize them significantly less) than the EC group, then the coefficient, α_8, will be significantly greater than zero.[q]

Since the sample is drawn from three different industries which may

---

[p] This statistical procedure is discussed in several econometrics textbooks. See, for example, Johnston [56, Ch. 6] and Kmenta [63, Ch. 11].

[q] Comparisons between OM and MC groups will also be obtained by substituting the EC dummy variable for the MC dummy variable in (4.3). Then the coefficient of the OM terms will represent the difference between the OM group and the MC group. Precisely the same tests could of course be obtained by contrasting OM and MC coefficients in (4.3).

exhibit different compensation structures, industry dummy variables will also be included to account for any inter-industry differences. The industry dummy variables are defined as follows:

$$D \begin{cases} = 1 \text{ if firm } i \text{ is in the drug industry} \\ = 0 \text{ otherwise} \end{cases}$$

$$L \begin{cases} = 1 \text{ if firm } i \text{ is in the petroleum industry} \\ = 0 \text{ otherwise} \end{cases}$$

When both D and L are zero the firm is in the chemical industry. With the addition of industry intercept and slope dummy variables the regression is as shown in expression (4.4):

$$C_i = \alpha_0 + \alpha_1 OM + \alpha_2 MC + \alpha_3 D + \alpha_4 L + \alpha_5 P_i + \alpha_6 OMP_i \\ + \alpha_7 MCP_i + \alpha_8 DP_i + \alpha_9 LP_i + \alpha_{10} S_i + \alpha_{11} OMS_i \\ + \alpha_{12} MCS_i + \alpha_{13} DS_i + \alpha_{14} LS_i + \mu_i. \qquad (4.4)$$

The revised expression now contains intercept and slope terms for both the type of control and the industry. Another regression will be run in which the firm's market value (V_i) is substituted for profits in (4.4) and is shown as follows:

$$C_i = \beta_0 + \beta_1 OM + \beta_2 MC + \beta_3 D + \beta_4 L + \beta_5 V_i + \beta_6 OMV_i \\ + \beta_7 MCV_i + \beta_8 DV_i + \beta_9 LV_i + \beta_{10} S_i + \beta_{11} OMS_i \\ + \beta_{12} MCS_i + \beta_{13} DS_i + \beta_{14} LS_i + \omega_i. \qquad (4.5)$$

There are statistical problems associated with the direct application of least squares regression analysis to equations (4.4) and (4.5). As with all previous cross-section research, a major obstacle is that both sales and profits (or market value) tend to move together, resulting in a high degree of collinearity between these two explanatory variables. This multicollinearity makes it impossible to sort our their individual effects. Another problem also encountered in earlier research [73, p. 713] was that the error term tended to increase with the magnitude of the dependent variable, thereby undermining the homoscedasticity assumption that the variance of the disturbance term is constant.[r] An approach adopted previously by Lewellen and Huntsman [73] that addressed both the problems of multicollinearity and heteroscedasticity is the use of a weighted regression technique, which requires some grounds for expecting that some scale-related deflator has a proportional relationship to the variances of the error terms. A

---
[r] If the constant variance assumption does not hold then the estimates of the coefficients derived from ordinary least squares are unbiased estimates of the true parameters, but the variances of the estimates may either understate or overstate the true variances.

weighting procedure which appears to correct for the problem of heteroscedasticity while also reducing multicollinearity is to divide all terms in the equation by the firm's net worth or equity (E_i) as in (4.6) and (4.7):[s]

$$C_i/E_i = \alpha_0(1/E_i) + \alpha_1(OM/E_i) + \alpha_2(MC/E_i) + \alpha_3(D/E_i)$$
$$+ \alpha_4(L/E_i) + \alpha_5(P_i/E_i) + \alpha_6(OMP_i/E_i) + \alpha_7(MCP_i/E_i)$$
$$+ \alpha_8(DP_i/E_i) + \alpha_9(LP_i/E_i) + \alpha_{10}(S_i/E_i) + \alpha_{11}(OMS_i/E_i)$$
$$+ \alpha_{12}(MCS_i/E_i) + \alpha_{13}(DS_i/E_i) + \alpha_{14}(LS_i/E_i) + \mu_i'. \quad (4.6)$$

The equation using market value as the stockholder welfare variable (4.7) is identical to (4.6) except V_i is substituted for P_i:[t]

$$C_i/E_i = \beta_0(1/E_i) + \beta_1(OM/E_i) + \beta_2(MC/E_i) + \beta_3(D/E_i)$$
$$+ \beta_4(L/E_i) + \beta_5(V_i/E_i) + \beta_6(OMV_i/E_i) + \beta_7(MCV_i/E_i)$$
$$+ \beta_8(DV_i/E_i) + \beta_9(LV_i/E_i) + \beta_{10}(S_i/E_i) + \beta_{11}(OMS_i/E_i)$$
$$+ \beta_{12}(MCS_i/E_i) + \beta_{13}(DS_i/E_i) + \beta_4(LS_i/E_i) + \omega_i'. \quad (4.7)$$

Hypotheses and Test Results

The implications developed in the second section concerning differences in compensation structures among control types plus some additional implications concerning differences based on the market power of the industry will now be presented as explicit hypotheses in terms of the coefficients of (4.6) and (4.7). There are four sets of hypotheses to be presented—two sets involve differences based on the control condition and two involve differences based on the industry. Each set will be discussed separately. A summary table of the predicted signs will follow the discussion.

---

[s] If the variances of the equity terms are roughly proportional to those of the disturbance terms in (4.4) and (4.5), we would expect the variances of the new error term $(\mu_i' = \mu_i/E_i)$ to be approximately constant over the sampling range. An examination of the scatter diagrams indicates that the least square assumption concerning the constancy of the error variance appears to be met in (4.6) and (4.7) for both the salary plus bonus and the total after-tax definitions of compensation. In accordance with our correction for heteroscedasticity the equations are estimated to pass through the origin. In order to check this specification we first ran the regressions with the constant term added (since all variables are multiplied by $1/E_i$, the constant term was added simply by including E_i as an additional explanatory variable, making the new term $E_i(1/E_i) = 1$). In no case was the constant term significantly different from zero, indicating that our correction for heteroscedasticity was effective. See Hall and Weiss [50, p. 324] for a discussion of this correction procedure.

[t] There is some economic appeal to using the firm's equity as a deflator because the result can be given an economic interpretation. The manager can now be thought of as maximizing company profits, market value, or sales per dollar of resources put at his disposal by the stockholders. The profits term becomes the ratio of net income to net worth and the market value term becomes market value to net worth, which is the Marris valuation ratio.

Hypotheses. Four sets of hypotheses are presented here.

I. Of primary interest here is the relationship of the compensation structures between the EC and MC firms. There are three hypotheses to be tested concerning differences in compensation structures between the EC and MC firms. The first is that EC managers are paid more compensation for profits and for market value than managers in MC firms ($\alpha_7 < 0, \beta_7 < 0$). Secondly, MC managers are paid more (penalized less) for sales, *ceteris paribus*, than managers in EC firms ($\alpha_{12} > 0, \beta_{12} > 0$). And, finally, to the extent that there are nonpecuniary advantages in working for MC firms, advantages that are competed away through lower levels of compensation paid to managers in those firms, then MC firms will exhibit a lower level of compensation than EC firms ($\alpha_2 < 0, \beta_2 < 0$).[u]

II. The differences between the OM and EC firms are not as clear. To the extent that the owner-managers pursue size we should expect the compensation structure in the OM groups to be more similar to the MC group than to the EC group. But to the extent that the owner-managers pay themselves incentives to maximize stockholder-welfare variables (and recall that other executives, at lower layers in the organization, face these incentives as well), then the owner-managers' compensation structure will be more similar to that in the EC firms. Thus the null hypothesis is that there is no difference in compensation packages between OM and EC firms, against the one-sided alternative hypothesis that the incentive structures in OM firms will differ from those in EC firms to look more like those in the MC group. The predicted signs for the alternative hypotheses are therefore the same as those predicted for the MC group.

III. Additional hypotheses can be developed to test whether the degree of barriers to entry per se has an impact on the manager's ability to manipulate his compensation structure. A general proposition is that the higher the barriers to entry, the more insulated the firm is from competition in the product market, and *ceteris paribus*, the more discretion the manager has in structuring his compensation. The more discretion available to a manager the more we expect the manager will tie his income to firm size and the less he will tie it to profits and market value. The drug industry has been defined as having "very high" entry barriers while both petroleum and chemicals are rated as having "substantial" barriers [78]. Since the drug industry has higher entry barriers than petroleum or chemicals, one might expect managers in the drug industry will be able to tie their income more to sales and less to profits than in either of the two industries. To the extent

---
[u] But since differences in the slope coefficients are being accounted for as well, we should exercise some care in interpreting the intercept terms, for it is not necessarily the case that if some executive in a particular industry or a particular control type has a lower intercept term then this group has a lower level of compensation over the entire range. Of course if there were no dummy variables for the slope terms then we could say that differences in the intercept term hold over the entire range.

that there are nonpecuniary advantages to working in the drug industry (e.g., more security because of greater insulation from the product market constraints) and these advantages are competed away, there should be a lower level of compensation for managers of the firms in this industry. These hypotheses can now be translated into predicted signs in (4.6) and (4.7). First, managers' compensation schemes in the drug industry are tied less to profits and market values than those in the chemical industry ($\alpha_8 < 0$, $\beta_8 < 0$). Second, managers' compensation schemes in the drug industry are tied more to sales than those in the chemical industry ($\alpha_{13} > 0$, $\beta_{13} > 0$). And, finally, to the extent that there are nonpecuniary advantages to working in the drug industry versus the chemical industry and they are bid away by competition among executives for more attractive jobs, compensation levels will be lower in the drug industry ($\alpha_3 < 0$, $\beta_3 < 0$).

IV. Since the chemical and petroleum industries have the same barriers to entry then neither is more insulated from product-market constraints. Hence we should expect to observe no difference in the way managers are paid for profits and market value ($\alpha_9 = 0, \beta_3 = 0$) or sales ($\alpha_{14} = 0, \beta_{14} = 0$). And if there are no nonpecuniary advantages to working in one industry over working in the other industry then the overall level of compensation should not differ significantly ($\alpha_4 = 0, \beta_4 = 0$).

It should be noted that none of these sets of hypotheses has been tested before, since no previous examination of control has sorted firms into the three control categories employed here, nor have firms been sorted into industries so that effects of market structure can also be examined. The four sets of hypotheses are summarized in table 4-2.

Results. Equations (4.6) and (4.7) were estimated using both before-tax salary plus bonus and full after-tax compensation as dependent variables. In addition to testing the sign and significance of each coefficient, an analysis of variance test was applied to each set of control-type and industry-type dummy variable to see whether, for example, the MC dummy variables jointly explain a significant amount of variation in executive compensation across firms. The procedure here is to estimate the coefficients in (4.6) and (4.7) including the dummy variables in question, then to run the regressions again with those terms constrained to equal zero. The standard errors of the estimates in each regression can then be used to compute an F-ratio.[v]

---

[v] Note that this particular F-test is not equivalent to testing individually whether each of the coefficients is zero. None of the coefficients may be significantly different from zero based on t-tests, yet the F-test may lead one to conclude that not all of the coefficients are zero. The individual estimates of any subset of coefficients are not necessarily independent of one another and in testing them simultaneously, the F-test takes this interdependence into account.

Table 4-2
Predicted Signs of the Four Sets of Hypotheses

Hypothesis		Term	Predicted Sign
Ia	α_7	MC vs. EC Profits	−
Ia	β_7	MC vs. EC Market Value	−
Ib	α_{12}, β_{12}	MC vs. EC Sales	+
Ib	α_2, β_2	MC vs. EC Intercept	−
IIa	α_6	OM vs. EC Profits	−
IIa	β_6	OM vs. EC Market Value	−
IIb	α_{11}, β_{11}	OM vs. EC Sales	+
IIc	α_1, β_1	OM vs. EC Intercept	−
IIIa	α_8	Drug vs. Chemical Profits	−
IIIa	β_8	Drug vs. Chemical Market Value	−
IIIb	α_{13}, β_{13}	Drug vs. Chemical Sales	+
IIIc	α_3, β_3	Drug vs. Chemical Intercept	−
IVa	α_9	Petroleum vs. Chemical Profits	0
IVa	β_9	Petroleum vs. Chemical Market Value	0
IVb	α_{14}, β_{14}	Petroleum vs. Chemical Sales	0
IVc	α_4, β_4	Petroleum vs. Chemical Intercept	0

Since the set of Hypotheses IV, involving the petroleum industry, predicts that this group of coefficients is not significantly different from zero (i.e., not significantly different from the coefficients of the chemical group), suggesting that we may want to drop them from the regression before proceeding, this group was examined first. In all regressions the coefficient of the slope terms (i.e., α_9, β_9, $\alpha_{14}\beta_{14}$) were never significantly different from zero. Moreover, as F-test for these terms also indicated that together they were not significantly different from zero, suggesting that these terms could be omitted without loss of significant explanatory power. With respect to the petroleum intercept terms (i.e., α_4, β_4), the coefficients for these terms were significantly different from zero when the simple definition (before-tax salary plus bonus) of compensation was used, but they were not significantly different from zero when the fuller definition (total after-tax compensation) was employed.[w] Thus the set of Hypotheses IV, that managers in the petroleum industry do not have compensation structures that differ significantly from the compensation structures in the chemical industry, can only be accepted when the full after-tax definition of compensation is the dependent variable. When salary plus bonus is used,

---
[w] When the fuller definition of compensation in the dependent variable the F-test for both intercept and slope terms indicates that none of the coefficients is significantly different from zero.

the managers in the two groups are not paid significantly different for profits, market value, and sales, but the level of compensation does differ significantly between the two industries. Since none of the petroleum terms differed significantly from zero when the full definition of compensation was used, and since the petroleum slope coefficients did not differ significantly from zero when salary plus bonus was used, these terms were omitted from (4.6) and (4.7) leaving the intercept term when salary-plus-bonus is the dependent variable as the only petroleum term in the expression.

Thus we need now be concerned with only the three remaining sets of hypotheses. The results of least squares regression on (4.6) using both definitions of compensation are given as (4.8) and (4.10), and the results of (4.7) are given as (4.9) and (4.11).

$$C = 142.70 - 42.47\,\text{OM} - 48.55\,\text{MC} - 4.77\,\text{D}$$
$$(8.90) \quad (-2.18) \quad\quad (-2.78) \quad\quad (-0.33)$$

$$- 72.65\,L + 1.67\,P - 1.40\,\text{OM}P - 1.17\,\text{MC}P$$
$$(-5.07) \quad (2.45) \quad\quad (-1.31) \quad\quad (-1.51)$$

$$- 1.00\,\text{D}P - 0.06\,S + 0.17\,\text{OM}S + 0.13\,\text{MC}S + 0.11\,\text{D}S \quad\quad (4.8)$$
$$(-1.35) \quad\quad (-1.29) \quad (2.03) \quad\quad\quad (2.55) \quad\quad\quad (1.73)$$

$R_a^2 = .944 \quad F = 67.07$

$$C = 121.00 - 77.06\,\text{OM} - 35.52\,\text{MC} + 20.81\,\text{D}$$
$$(6.99) \quad (-3.06) \quad\quad (-2.02) \quad\quad (1.17)$$

$$- 47.13\,L + 0.075\,V - 0.004\,\text{OM}V - 0.047\,\text{MC}V$$
$$(-2.88) \quad (3.12) \quad\quad (-0.12) \quad\quad\quad (-2.19)$$

$$- 0.060\,\text{D}V - 0.041\,S + 0.164\,\text{OM}S + .120\,\text{MC}S$$
$$(-2.56) \quad\quad (-1.22) \quad (3.33) \quad\quad\quad (3.42)$$

$$+ .118\,\text{D}S \quad\quad\quad\quad\quad\quad\quad\quad\quad\quad\quad\quad\quad\quad (4.9)$$
$$(2.18)$$

$R_a^2 = .955 \quad F = 83.51$

$$C^* = 250.90 + 92.21\,\text{OM} - 152.80\,\text{MC} - 123.20\,\text{D}$$
$$(9.25) \quad\quad (1.95) \quad\quad\quad (-4.70) \quad\quad\quad (-3.43)$$

$$+ 12.57\,P - 3.97\,\text{OM}P - 9.89\,\text{MC}P - 9.74\,\text{D}P$$
$$(6.52) \quad\quad (-1.25) \quad\quad (-4.56) \quad\quad (-4.63)$$

$$- 0.977\,S + 0.041\,\text{OM}S + 0.943\,\text{MC}S + 0.960\,\text{D}S \quad\quad (4.10)$$
$$(-7.27) \quad (0.17) \quad\quad\quad (6.34) \quad\quad\quad\quad (5.01)$$

$R_a^2 = .881 \quad F = 32.73$

$$C^* = 266.50 - 36.87\,\text{OM} - 247.90\,\text{MC} - 46.14\,\text{D}$$
$$(10.00) \quad (-0.50) \quad\;\; (-6.16) \quad\;\; (-1.08)$$

$$+\; 0.364\,V - 0.133\,\text{OM}V - 0.143\,\text{MC}V - 0.270\,\text{D}V$$
$$(6.23) \quad\;\; (-1.48) \quad\quad (-2.24) \quad\quad (-4.75)$$

$$-\; 0.659\,S + 0.345\,\text{OM}S + 0.676\,\text{MC}S + 0.421\,\text{D}S \qquad (4.11)$$
$$(6.35) \quad\;\; (2.11) \quad\quad\;\; (6.02) \quad\quad\;\; (2.52)$$

$R_a^2 = .885 \qquad F = 34.05$

One-tailed tests are appropriate for the coefficients here since all have one-sided alternatives. The results for each hypothesis are summarized in table 4-3 where the predicted signs are compared with the t-values of the relevant coefficients. The F-values for each subset (e.g., MC) of dummy variables are also presented. The results for each set of hypotheses will be discussed in order.

I. All of the signs of the coefficients for the MC group are as predicted and all but one are significant at the 0.05 level or better (the remaining coefficient is significant at the 0.10 level). Moreover, the F-values indicate that we can reject the hypothesis that all the coefficients are equal to zero at the 0.001 level or better. Note that the hypothesis test here is not of MC coefficients with respect to zero but is a contrast of MC coefficients with respect to the coefficients for the EC group. Significance levels for both t- and F-values are consistently higher when the fuller definition of compensation is used. Thus the evidence is strong that managers in EC firms are paid more for stockholder welfare variables and less (penalized more) for sales than managers in MC firms. In addition, the nonpecuniary advantages of working in the MC firms bid down the level of pecuniary compensation in those firms, presumably because of competition among executives for these more attractive jobs.

II. Ten of the twelve signs of the OM coefficients are as predicted but significance levels are generally lower than with the MC coefficients. The coefficients of the profit and market value term are never significantly lower than the coefficient for the EC profit and market value term. The OM sales term has the predicted sign each time it appears and is significant at least at the 0.05 level three out of four times, suggesting that owner-managers may pay themselves more for sales than managers in EC firms are paid. The OM intercept term has the predicted sign three of four times, and is significant at least at the 0.025 level twice. In general the EC and OM compensation structures appear to differ more when the salary-plus-bonus definition of compensation is employed; the F-values when this definition of compensation is used are significant at the 0.0005 level, but when the full after-tax value of compensation is employed the F-value is significant at the 0.05 level only when market value is the stockholder welfare variable. Thus

Table 4-3
Significance Levels Based on T and F Tests

			T-Values			
			Salary plus Bonus		Full After-Tax	
Hypothesis and Predicted Sign			(4.8)	(4.9)	(4.10)	(4.11)
Ia. MC vs EC Profits	α_7	−	−1.51		−4.56[e]	
Ia. MC vs EC Mkt. Value	β_7	−		−2.19[b]		−2.24[b]
Ib. MC vs EC Sales	α_{12}, β_{12}	+	2.55[c]	3.42[c]	6.34[e]	6.02[e]
Ic. MC vs EC Intercept	α_2, β_2	−	−2.78[c]	−2.02[a]	−4.70[e]	−6.16[e]
Joint Test (F-Values)		+	(7.21)[d]	(8.37)[e]	(21.05)[e]	(23.91)[e]
IIa. OM vs. EC Profits	α_6	−	−1.31		−1.25	
IIa. OM vs EC Mkt. Value	β_6	−		−0.12		−1.48
IIb. OM vs EC Sales	α_{11}, β_{11}	+	2.03[a]	3.33[c]	0.17	2.11[b]
IIc. OM vs EC Intercept	α_1, β_1	−	−2.18[b]	−3.06[c]	1.95	−0.50
Joint Test (F-Values)		+	(7.69)[e]	(10.86)[e]	(2.35)	(3.76)[a]
IIIa. Drug Profits	α_8	−	−1.35		−4.63[e]	
IIIa. Drug Mkt. Value	β_8	−		−2.56[c]		−4.75[e]
IIIb. Drug Sales	α_{13}, β_{13}	+	1.73[a]	2.18[b]	5.01[e]	2.52[c]
IIIc. Drug Intercept	α_3, β_3	−	−0.33	1.17	−3.43[d]	−1.08
Joint Test (F-Values)		+	(2.09)	(3.80)[a]	(15.83)[e]	(13.57)[e]
	R_a^2		.944	.955	.881	.885
	F		67.07[e]	83.52[e]	32.73[e]	34.04[e]

[a] — significant at .05 level
[b] — significant at .025 level
[c] — significant at .01 level
[d] — significant at .001 level
[e] — significant at .0005 level

when all sources of pecuniary compensation are included, the owner-managers' pay structure appears more like the EC structure, the structure designed to elicit profit-maximizing behavior from managers.

It might also be helpful to compare the OM group with the MC group. To do this a set of EC dummy variables was substituted for the set of MC dummy variables so that OM and EC became the two control dummy variables (when both were equal to zero the firm was MC). This permits direct and clear comparisons between the OM and MC firms. Although no hypothesis was explicitly developed concerning the relationship between compensation structures in these two groups, since we assumed that the two groups had the same predicted signs with respect to the EC group (i.e.,

Hypotheses I and II) then to be consistent we formulate the null hypothesis as stating the OM and MC groups have compensation structures which do not differ significantly against the one-sided alternative that owner-managers are more similar to the EC group and are therefore paid more for stockholder welfare variables, less for sales, and more overall than managers in MC firms.

The t-values for each coefficient and the F-values for each subset of coefficients are reported in table 4-4 for comparisons between the OM and MC groups. Of course, the values of all other parameters are the same as in table 4-3 with the exception that the coefficients of the EC group are identical to the MC coefficients in table 4-3, but with opposite signs (since these two groups simply switch places in the equation). When salary plus bonus is the definition of compensation, the OM and MC groups appear to have the same compensation structure; no coefficient is significant and no F-value is significant, suggesting that all coefficients are equal to zero. (Since the null hypothesis in each instance has a one-sided alternative, all significance levels apply to one-tailed tests.) But when the fuller definition of income is employed, the owner-managers have a compensation structure significantly different from the MC group. All signs then are as predicted by the alternative hypothesis and seven of eight are significant at the 0.05 level or better. The F-values are significant at the 0.0005 level.

This result mirrors the comparison of the OM and EC group. There the compensation structures differed most when the salary-plus-bonus definition of compensation was used, but when the full after-tax value of compensation was used the OM and EC compensation structures appeared more similar. When the value of all compensation is considered the owner-managers appear to have a compensation structure that is designed more to maximize stockholder welfare than is the structure in the MC firms.

III. The results for the high-entry-barrier drug industry group are generally as predicted; eleven of the twelve signs are as predicted and eight of eleven are significant at the 0.05 level or better. Three of the four stockholder-welfare variables confirm at the 0.01 level or better the hypothesis that compensation in drug firms is tied less to stockholder-welfare variables than it is in chemical firms. All four of the sales coefficients are significant indicating that managers in drug firms are paid more for sales, *ceteris paribus*, than managers in chemical firms. The drug intercept term is negative, as predicted, three of the four times, but it is significant only once. Again the results of an F-test indicate that differences between the drug and petroleum groups are more marked when the fuller definition of compensation is used. The F-value is significant in three of the four cases, and is significant at the 0.0005 level when the more complete definition of compensation is employed.

Table 4-4
Comparison of OM and MC Firms

Hypothesis and Predicted Sign		T-Values			
		Salary plus Bonus		Full After-Tax	
II'a. OM vs MC profits	+	0.20		1.69[a]	
II'a. OM vs MC Mkt. Value	+		1.53		0.10
II'b. OM vs MC Sales	−	0.47	1.07	−3.62[c]	−2.45[b]
II'c. OM vs MC Intercept	+	0.40	−1.76	5.39[d]	2.72[b]
Joint Test (F-Value)	+	(1.39)	(2.31)	(24.34)[d]	(10.39)[d]

[a]—significant at .05 level
[b]—significant at .01 level
[c]—significant at .001 level
[d]—significant at .0005 level

The adjusted R^2 drops slightly when the fuller definition of compensation is substituted as dependent variable for salary plus bonus, but the overall level in each regression is high, particularly for a cross-section study. With profits as the stockholder-welfare variable the R^2 dropped from 0.944 with salary-plus-bonus to 0.881 with full after-tax compensation. With market value as the stockholder-welfare variable the R^2 dropped from 0.955 to 0.885. This drop is consistent with the results of Lewellen and Huntsman [73] where there also appeared to be a loss in explanatory power in going to the fuller definition of compensation. They presented two possible explanations for this result. The first was the somewhat tautological argument that the model using only salary plus bonus performed "substantially better than anticipated, leaving relatively little room for improvement" [73, p. 717]. The second argument was that a part of the fuller definition consists of some equity-related income (i.e., stock options), which reflects more random factors [73, p. 718]. Another possible explanation is the arbitrary nature of tax and present value calculations necessary to estimate full after-tax income. (In spite of the drop in explanatory power these results are considerably better than those in any previous research.)

These results are not inconsistent with any earlier findings; they simply take the analysis further. For example, when Larner looked at a subsample of manager-controlled firms, he found that this subsample was not paid for sales, *ceteris paribus*. The results here do not say that the MC group is paid for sales, they say only that the MC managers are paid significantly more (penalized less) for sales than the EC managers. Likewise, Larner found that the MC group was paid for profits; the above analysis notes only that the MC group is paid less for profits than the EC group.

O.E. Williamson, using the internal composition of the board as a proxy for management control, found in one of the three years he examined that firms with a higher internal representation had significantly higher level of salaries [139, pp. 133-35]. If the internal composition of the board had yielded a true indicator of management control, then Williamson's results might tend to contradict the view that the advantages of employment in an MC firm are competed away by a lower salary.[x] To test for the actual relationship between internal representation on the board and the control type based on the distribution of shares, a sample of 96 firms was selected randomly from the "*Forbes* Five Hundreds."[y] Of this sample the firms with a dominant stockholding interest—whether as part of management or outside the firm—had a significantly higher proportion of managers on the board of directors.[z] Thus the firms Williamson identified as manager-controlled firms are more likely to be firms with a dominant stockholder, and it is this group of firms that displayed a higher level of salary. The conclusions he draws from this evidence concerning managerial discretion may therefore be incorrect [139, p. 134], because what he considered MC firms probably were either EC or OM firms instead.

Job Tenure Based on Control

An examination of pay incentives looks at the "carrot" that the manager faces; the possibility of being fired represents the "stick" that confronts him. Alchian suggests that if the management in manager-controlled firms is in fact the monolithic group with no interpersonal rivalries implied by the discretionary theories, then we should observe longer tenures for managers in firms without a dominant stockholder [1, p. 341]. Alchian envisions firms as being divided into those with "dispersed ownership" and those that are closely held. Apparently the closely held firms can do a better job of

---

[x] Although our intercept term is not strictly comparable with Williamson's intercept term because we allowed the slope coefficients to vary with control as well and they did not.

[y] The sample was stratified so that there were 32 MC firms, 32 EC firms and 32 OM firms. All were taken from the *Forbes* list [39] as of 1972.

[z] In quantitative terms, the presence of a dominant interest can be translated into increasing the proportion of insiders by 10 percent of the total board. Similar results were also found using Larner's sample of the top 200 firms [57]. The reasons for such a link are not immediately clear. It may be that a dominant stockholder feels he has more control over a manager whom he can fire at any time than over an outside board member such as a banker who may attempt to represent other interests. P.C. Dooley examined the composition of boards [35] and found that as firms became less solvent, the internal representation on the board of directors declined, and the number of interlocks particularly with sources of credit increased. Hence, if the manager-controlled firms as a group were less solvent, this may explain the lower internal representation. Another *ad hoc* explanation is that manager-controlled firms are more anxious to give stockholders the impression that rather than a closed group, their firm is a wide-open operation subject to the scrutiny of mostly outsiders. The presence of outsiders on the board is often stressed by management particularly during proxy contests and unwelcome tender offers.

policing their managers and hence we should find a shorter tenure in those firms. But such a view ignores the fact that many closely held firms also are owner-managed. Who is going to police the owner-manager? Shouldn't we expect this manager to be able to weather any rough period, and be able to keep his job when managers in EC or even MC firms would be dismissed? And even if we grant that the world consists of only EC and MC firms, Alchian's argument does not necessarily hold up. The apparent rationale behind this view is that since the transaction costs of replacing the manager are lower in EC firms, these managers will experience shorter tenures. This implication would be correct if the managers in both EC and MC firms attempted to divert profits to the same extent, even though the EC managers had less room for discretion. But if the manager in each group operates within the constraints imposed on him, there is no reason to expect one to be fired any more frequently than the other.

One way to compare job tenures is simply to look at the average length of time that executives of each control type have been in office. This was done for both the industry sample and the larger sample consisting of 32 firms in each control type.[aa] The form of the regression for the industry sample is as follows:

$$E_i = \theta_0 + \theta_1 \text{OM} + \theta_2 \text{MC} + \theta_3 \text{D} + \theta_4 \text{L} + \mu_i, \quad (4.12)$$

where E_i is the years spent as chief executive for the manager in firm i as of December 1972, OM and MC are type-of-control dummy variables, D and L are drug and petroleum industry dummy variables, and μ_i is the random disturbance term with mean zero and variance σ_μ^2. The null hypothesis is that there is no difference in tenure between EC and OM firms ($\theta_1 = 0$), against the one-sided alternative that owner-managers, because of their larger holdings in the firm, have a greater ability to keep their jobs and therefore experience longer tenures ($\theta_1 > 0$). A second hypothesis, suggested by Alchian, is that managers in MC firms are better able to keep their jobs than managers in EC firms, who are more closely supervised ($\theta_2 > 0$). Estimates based on data from the 48 firms in the industry sample are as follows:

$$E = 5.68 + 11.44\,\text{OM} + 0.65\,\text{MC} + 0.027\,\text{D} - 0.41\,\text{L} \quad (4.13)$$
$$\quad (2.02)\ (3.34) \qquad (0.24) \qquad (0.74) \qquad (-0.15)$$

$R_a^2 = .19 \qquad F = 3.67$

The OM group appear to have an average tenure nearly twice that of the other two categories, and the difference between the EC and OM group is significant at the 0.001 level. The MC dummy variable has the predicted

---

[aa] Since the large sample was drawn randomly it includes some of the same firms that appeared in the industry sample. About 18 percent of the firms in the large sample appear in the industry sample as well.

sign although it is not significant, indicating the null hypothesis that the two groups have similar tenures cannot be rejected. The same hypothesis will be tested for the larger, 96-firm, sample. Since the industry terms were not significant in (4.13) there is some justification for using the type-of-control variables as the only explanatory variables. This was done and the results are given as follows:

$$E = 4.59 + 10.97\,\text{OM} + 0.12\,\text{MC} \qquad (4.14)$$
$$(3.83)\quad(6.46)\qquad(0.07)$$

$R_a^2 = .36 \qquad F = 27.58$

The job tenure of the owner-managed group is again about twice the other two groups, and is highly significant. The sign of the MC dummy variable is correct but there is no significant difference in job tenure between EC and MC firms. Thus it does not appear that EC managers are fired with any more frequency than are executives in MC firms, but owner-managers, on average, have been in office about twice as long as the others.

Sorenson's work on job tenure is the only research with which our findings might be compared [125]. Recall that he sorted firms into owner-controlled and manager-controlled categories and found the manager-controlled firms had higher turnover rates. The turnover rate is nothing more than the reciprocal of our average tenure term. If we converted our average tenure figures into turnover rates, the turnover rates between EC and MC firms would not differ significantly. But if we compared MC groups with all owner-controlled firms (i.e., OM plus EC firms), then the MC group would appear to have the higher turnover rate since the longer tenure in the OM group would lower the average turnover rate of the owner-controlled firms. This may very well be the explanation for what Sorenson observed. Although Sorenson's results have been interpreted as showing "that the penalty for failure . . . is significantly greater in manager-controlled firms" [19, p. 2], such conclusions appear misleading when one realizes that the owner-controlled group consists not only of hired managers but also of owner managers, and it really is the latter group that creates the difference in turnover rates between owner-controlled and manager-controlled firms.

Summary and Conclusions

The first section of this chapter examined the positive and negative incentives facing the manager in each of three control types. The incentive structures of managers in EC firms appeared to be more designed to maximize profits and market value than the structure in manager-controlled firms. Managers in EC firms were paid more for profits and market value and less (penalized more) for sales, *ceteris paribus,* than managers in MC firms. Also it appeared that the advantages of working in an MC firm were competed away, to some extent, resulting in a lower level of compensation in these firms. The OM group had a salary structure similar to the MC group when the simple definition of compensation was used, but when the full after-tax compensation was used, the OM structure more resembled the structure in EC firms. The industry dummy variables indicated that firms in the drug industry, which had higher barriers to entry, were more able than firms in the other industries to lever executive compensation away from profits and market value and more toward sales. But the petroleum industry, which had the same barriers to entry as the chemical industry, had the same compensation structure as the chemical industry with respect to profits, market value, and sales. This inter-industry difference in compensation structures suggests that previous research on compensation which neglected industry effects may have left out some important information.

The tenure of the top executives based on the control situation was also examined. Tenure did not differ between EC and MC firms, suggesting that the managers in both types of firms had similar respect for the bounds of their ranges of discretionary activity. But the owner-managers were more able to keep their jobs and had average tenures about twice as long as the other two.

5 Management Performance Under Three Control Conditions

Introduction

The incentives facing the manager under each of three control conditions were examined in the previous chapter. The compensation structure of externally-controlled firms appeared to be designed more to maximize profits and market value than the compensation structure in manager-controlled firms. Externally-controlled managers were paid more for profits and less for sales, *ceteris paribus*, than managers in manager-controlled firms. In view of these differences, an appropriate question to ask is what impact do the different compensation schemes have on firm performance. More specifically, is a stockholder's investment better utilized when the manager is rewarded more for profits and market value? In the second section we shall examine differences in the rate of return on a stockholder's investment based on the three control conditions, using the same sample of 48 firms in three industries from Chapter 4. In the third and fourth sections two related questions concerning managerial performance will be discussed: Does the control condition affect either the firm's retention policy (third section) or the firm's risk (fourth section)? Past empirical work has found significant but *opposite* results concerning the impact of control condition on these two performance variables. It will be shown that using the threefold definition of control clears up much of the confusion found in these earlier studies. The final section will briefly summarize the findings.

Stockholder Welfare Based on Three Control Conditions

The last chapter examined the compensation structure facing managers; the question remaining is what impact does this structure of incentives have on stockholder welfare. Do the financial incentives in externally-controlled firms motivate the manager to perform more in the stockholders' interest? Nearly all of the studies discussed in Chapter 3 which attempted to look at differences in performance viewed the firm's rate of return to equity as the appropriate stockholder-welfare variable. This exclusive reliance on rate of return to equity was criticized for several reasons. First, simply looking at the rate of return to equity neglects any treatment of the risk associated with that firm. As De Alessi points out, different rates of return may simply represent different capital structures [33]. Focusing on only the rate of return to equity also ignores the dividend policy in a firm; as Gordon notes, stockholders must be able to claim profits [48, p. 236]. A more appropriate variable, which takes into account both the riskiness of the firm's stream of returns and the firm's dividend policy, is the market value of a firm's share. And the variable that translates most directly into the stockholder's welfare is the rate of return experienced on a stock purchased and held over some period of time.

Alchian asks if stockholders in closely-held firms experienced a higher rate of growth in their wealth (including dividends and capital gains) than stockholders in "dispersed ownership firms" [1, pp. 347-48]. The performance variable selected for this analysis was the combined rate of return, considering all dividends as reinvested, on a share of stock over the ten-year period 1963 to 1972. From the stockholder's point of view this represents the most important performance characteristic of the firm. Yet there still is one major problem with this measure of performance: to the extent that the manager's incentive structure has already been capitalized in the value of a firm's shares (that is, firms with compensation structures levered more towards stockholder-welfare variables and less towards sales are valued more in the stock market), the control type will not appear to have much of an effect over time. In a sense, such a test is too severe. It is asking the manager in the EC firm not only to do better, but to do continually better than the market expects.

All previous studies examining performance based on control type have coupled EC firms and OM firms and compared them as a group to MC firms. This can be done with the sample simply by regressing the combined rate of return onto an MC dummy variable. The control dummy variable is defined as follows:

$$\text{MC} \begin{cases} = 1 \text{ if firm } i \text{ is manager-controlled} \\ = 0 \text{ elsewhere} \end{cases}$$

When MC is zero the firm is either externally-controlled or owner-managed. The industry dummy variables are also included to account for inter-industry differences in performance over the period and are defined as follows:

$$\text{D} \begin{cases} = 1 \text{ if firm } i \text{ is in the drug industry} \\ = 0 \text{ otherwise} \end{cases}$$

$$\text{L} \begin{cases} = 1 \text{ if firm } i \text{ is in the petroleum industry} \\ = 0 \text{ otherwise} \end{cases}$$

When both D and L are zero the firm is in the chemical industry. The regression equation is:

$$G_i = \gamma_0 + \gamma_1 MC + \gamma_2 D_i + \gamma_3 L_i + \mu_i, \qquad (5.1)$$

where G_i is the combined rate of return for a share of stock in firm i between 1963 and 1972.[a] MC is the manager-controlled dummy variable, and D and L are drug and petroleum industry dummy variables. The null hypothesis is that there is no difference in the return to stockholders based on the type of control ($\gamma_1 = 0$), tested against the one-sided alternative that MC firms return less to stockholders than firms with a dominant stockholder ($\gamma_1 < 0$). The results are given in (5.2)

$$G = \underset{(4.58)}{12.24} - \underset{(-2.41)}{5.90 MC} + \underset{(1.67)}{5.01 D} + \underset{(2.01)}{5.96 L} \qquad (5.2)$$

$R_a^2 = .17 \qquad F = 4.21$

The MC group yielded a lower return, since the coefficient of the MC term is negative and significant at the 0.01 level. Stockholders who in 1963 purchased shares in firms with a dominant stockholder either as an outsider or as a manager and held onto those shares for ten years did significantly better than stockholders who purchased shares in MC firms.

A further breakdown to comply with the threefold control categories we have introduced involves dividing the dominant stockholder group into OM and EC firms. The control dummy variables to be introduced are as follows:

$$\text{OM} \begin{cases} = 1 \text{ if firm } i \text{ is owner-managed} \\ = 0 \text{ elsewhere} \end{cases}$$

$$\text{EC} \begin{cases} = 1 \text{ if firm } i \text{ is externally-controlled} \\ = 0 \text{ elsewhere} \end{cases}$$

When both OM and EC are zero the firm is manager-controlled. The industry dummy variables remain as in (5.1). The revised expression is as follows:

$$G_i = \delta_0 + \delta_1 OM + \delta_2 EC + \delta_3 D + \delta_4 L + \omega_i \qquad (5.3)$$

Again the null hypothesis is that the EC group returns the same rate of

---

[a] The combined earning includes both price appreciation and dividend yield to an investor in a company's stock. The calculation assumed sale at the end of 1972 of any stock owned at the end of 1962. It has been assumed that any proceeds from cash dividends, the sale of rights and warrant offerings, and stock received in spin-offs, were reinvested at the end of the year in which they were received. These returns are adjusted for stock splits, stock dividends, recapitalizations, and corporate reorganizations as they occurred; however, no effort was made to reflect the cost of brokerage commissions or taxes. The ten-year figures are averages compounded annually. The data for all but two firms were found in *Fortune* [40, June, 1973]. The combined earnings for one drug company (A.H. Robins, Inc.) was computed as of July of 1963 since earlier stock quotations were not available. One chemical company (Clorox, Inc.) had to be omitted since it was a wholly-owned subsidiary until January of 1969.

return to stockholders as the MC group ($\delta_2 = 0$) against the one-sided alternative that EC firms yeild higher returns ($\delta_2 > 0$). The estimates of the coefficients are:

$$G = 6.30 + 8.20\text{OM} + 4.57\text{EC} + 5.11\text{D} + 6.00\text{L} \qquad (5.4)$$
$$(2.77)(2.45)(1.64)(1.71)(2.02)$$

$R_a^2 = .17 \qquad F = 3.41$

The EC firms yield higher returns, as expected, but the effect would now be significant only at the 0.06 level. The OM group yields over twice the return of MC firms, however, and the difference between OM and MC firms remains significant at the 0.01 level.

These results say nothing more than that incentives work, but they are free of a large part of the identification problem found in earlier research. The analysis of compensation specifically excluded income from the manager's personal holdings in the firm. This was done to avoid the identification problem that can arise because in deciding on whether to own part of the firms they manage, managers might buy into the more successful firms and refuse to buy into firms which they feel will be less successful. For if they respond that way, there is a link between equity-related income and the performance variables, such as firm profitability and market value, which is in no way caused by the incentives managers face. Instead, firm performance is in part a cause of equity-related income structure and there is a simultaneous equation system calling for identification. Since equity income is not paid to the manager in his capacity as manager, but simply in his capacity as risk bearer, it was thought that the exclusion of this amount would not seriously distort results that were aimed at uncovering effects of compensation structures, and it would prevent any difficulty in establishing the direction of causation. In fact if this equity-related income had been included there is little doubt that it would have strengthened the findings concerning compensation structures. The EC managers held, on the average, more than twice the amount of stock as the managers in the MC firms in 1972 whether measured in terms of the fraction of the total issue or the market value of holdings. Combine this with the fact that the returns on a share of stock were significantly higher in EC firms and it suggests that the managers in these firms will be paid more overall for stockholder-related variables than managers in MC firms.

Moreover, the OM group, by definition, had a total income package tied much more to the firm's stock market performance than the MC group. Owner-managers held, on the average, more than eighty times the stock held by the MC group whether measured in terms of the fraction of the firm owned or the market value of the holdings. And this group of firms experienced a rate of return on stockholders' investment that was about twice the rate of the MC firms.

Recall that Masson, using both income from stock ownership plus other forms of income, found that firms which tied the manager's income more to the firm's market value displayed a higher return to stockholders. Masson neglected any consideration of the control condition, and by including equity-related income in his definition of compensation he failed to treat the identification problem we have described. Thus he may simply have been confirming the phenomenon that managers, because of inside information and stock options, may buy into more promising firms and refuse to buy into firms which they feel will be less successful. The evidence derived in this study concerning differences in compensation structures between EC and MC firms is stronger than Masson's because it is free of the bias resulting from the possibility that a link supposedly dependent on a stockholder-welfare variable actually can in part be affecting managers' income rather than the other way around as claimed.

Thus far it has been shown that the EC firms had compensation structures geared more to stockholder-welfare variables and less to size per se. In addition the above results indicate that firms with these incentive structures experienced higher rates of return to stockholders. It has also been shown that the three-part classification of control is a more logical way to look at compensation, tenure, and performance than the two-part division employed in previous analysis. The final two sections of this chapter will examine two additional performance characteristics of the firm which have been a source of confusion in past empirical work: the firm's risk and its retention policy.

Retention Policy Based on Control Type

Another implication of the alternative theories of the firm is that hired managers have a preference for retained earnings over dividends, because, it is argued, retained earnings represent a source of discretion [139] and provide funds for expansion of the firm plus expansion of all the non-pecuniary benefits that go with firm size [9; 44; 83]. Managers are envisioned as pushing investment programs to a point where the marginal rate of return is below the level which would maximize stockholder welfare. Retained earnings are particularly favored for expansion because they are so accessible and they don't force the firm into selling new securities or issuing debt in the capital market. In Chapter 3 it was noted, however, that the empirical studies viewing retention based on control appeared to conflict. O.E. Williamson, using the fraction of managers on the board of directors as a proxy for the degree of management control, found that firms with higher internal representation on the board retained a significantly higher fraction of earnings. He concluded that as internal representation increases, "stockholder interests are subordinated to managerial objectives" [139, p. 135]. But David Kamerschen, employing Larner's sample of the top 200 firms and Larner's definitions of control [58, p. 772], and our analysis of Sorenson's data [126, p. 147], both found manager-controlled firms retained significantly less earnings than firms with a dominant stockholder.

The Sorenson and Kamerschen studies have two major shortcomings. The first is that "owner-controlled" firms were taken to reflect the typical stockholder's view concerning retained earnings, when dominant stockholders are apt to be exceptionally wealthy. And primarily because of the tax laws, the dominant stockholder may view retained earnings more favorably than the average stockholder. Thus the way to test whether managers retain more earnings than stockholders would prefer is not necessarily to compare the retention policy of firms with a dominant stockholder to manager-controlled firms. After all, if dominant stockholders are more wealthy their higher tax bracket will make retained earnings more attractive relative to dividends. Thus the comparison could be biased due to tax effects which inevitably are different for the two groups of firms. Until quite recently the maximum tax rate applied to capital gains was 25 percent whereas the personal income tax had a marginal rate of more than twice this amount.[b] Moreover tax laws permit capital gains to escape taxes altogether if they are passed on at death, making retained earnings even more attractive. Since it seems reasonable to assume that the average dominant stockholder has owned shares in the firm over a longer period than the average stockholder (nearly all individual dominant stockholders either inherited their holdings or founded the firm), this group also is likely to have more incentive to hold onto the shares and pass them on at death. In addition, a lower but more consistent dividend yield is likely to be taxed less, on average, than a higher but more erratic yield. Studies have shown that people in higher tax brackets have a perference for stocks which pay a relatively low but steady dividend.[c] Finally, as Kamerschen notes [58, p. 670], the fear of loss of control may encourage the dominant stockholder to prefer retained earnings over new issues or debt as a source of growth. So although the hired managers' preference for retained earnings may be greater than the average stockholder's it may not necessarily exceed that of a dominant stockholder.

---

[b] The Tax Reform Act of 1969 issued a new maximum capital gains rate of 35 percent to go into effect gradually [106, pp. 93-96]. We should note, however, that Mueller has developed a simple model indicating that stockholders can enjoy the lower capital-gains tax rate by having management use earnings to repurchase some of the firm's stock [95, pp. 206-207].

[c] W.L. Crum found that the preferences of high income groups for securities paying a lower dividend is reflected by the higher concentration of ownership in these securities [28]. Edwin Cox obtained similar results. For a cross-section of 31 firms he correlated the dividend yield (dividend-price ratio) with the percentage of shares held by the top 5 percent of the stockholders and found a strong negative relationship [26].

A second problem with the Sorenson and Kamerschen analyses is that under the heading of owner-controlled firms were joined both EC and OM firms. But the owner-manager has access to the same discretionary aspects of retained earning that interest the hired manager, while the external owner has little access to these nonpecuniary aspects. The owner-manager's preference for retained earnings is therefore likely to be stronger than the external controller's. Economists long ago recognized that owner-managers frequently tend to expand the firm because of the nonpecuniary advantage derived from this activity. The views of Knight [64, p. 162], Schumpeter [113, p. 93], and Gordon [48, pp. 331-32] dealing with the owner-managers preference for empire building were discussed earlier. Even Marris concedes that the owner-manager may prefer to plow money back into the firm when "his personal financial position is not to be significantly improved" [83, p. 10]. For "there is nothing in the rules of traditional capitalism to require the owner-manager to exclude all forms of satisfaction other than money" [83, p. 10]. More recently Mueller has argued that although we usually view the pursuit of growth as confined to those instances where there exists a separation of ownership from control, "... this may often happen when the stockholder control group also includes some of the managers" [96, p. 679]. Thus owner-managers have the freedom and they may also have the incentive to pursue other-than-profit maximizing objectives.

The OM firms may have a greater preference for retained earnings than the EC or MC groups for other reasons, too. If we examined a cross-section of firms we might expect that those firms that still have an owner-manager are, on average, younger. As the firm becomes older, death and taxes reduce the probability of maintaining a descendant of the founding family as manager.[d] And there is evidence to suggest that younger firms grow faster and consequently have greater needs for capital.[e] Moreover, since

---

[d] For our industry sample a regression equation was estimated using the age of the firm as the dependent variable with control and industry dummy variables as explanatory variables. EC and MC dummy variables were used to account for differences in the type of control (i.e., when both EC and MC were zero, the firm was owner-managed). One might expect the OM group to be the youngest, with the EC group in the middle (since a sizable fraction stock is still in the hands of a single interest group), followed by the MC group. The results for the industry sample are as follows:

$$\text{Age} = 48.00 + 15.30 \text{ MC} + 9.59 \text{EC} + 19.71 \text{D} + 3.29 \text{L} \qquad (5.5)$$
$$(5.28) \quad (1.75) \qquad (1.01) \qquad (2.55) \quad (0.43)$$

$R_a^2 = .11 \qquad F = 2.46$

After accounting for the age of the industry through the industry dummy variables, the MC group is significantly older than the OM group; the EC group also is older, but this difference is not significant. But the overall explanatory power of the equation is low.

[e] Dennis Mueller has attempted to develop a "life cycle theory" of the firm in which the age of the firm plays an important role in predicting its capital needs and growth rate [95]. He cites evidence suggesting that age is a better explanatory variable than size in determining growth rates [95, p. 210].

OM firms are apt to be younger, it is more likely that the stock is less dispersed among members of the family than it is in the EC firms. The older the dominant-stockholder firm becomes, the more widely distributed the shares are among succeeding members of the family. This greater diffusion of stock for a given fraction of the firm would appear to make the tax advantages of retained earnings less attractive to the individual members of the family. The main implication of all of this is that for several reasons owner-managers have a greater preference for retained earnings than the dominant outside stockholders, so a distinction between these two control categories again is warranted.

Owner-managers may not only have a preference for retained earnings; they also have a wider range of discretion in dictating retention policy than hired managers. The research of Dennis Mueller and Henry G. Grabowski suggests that dividends are paid out by managers in part to keep the wolves away—to obtain security against a take-over [97]. They note that factors which diminish this threat such as an above-average growth rate in earnings per share also are associated with lower dividends, whereas factors like a more erratic earnings pattern actually will increase the possibility of a take-over and result in higher dividends [97, p. 20]. Since the owner-manager is by definition in control of the firm, he is free to retain an even larger fraction of earnings than managers in MC firms without fear of being replaced.

The retention ratio is obviously responsive to a number of considerations other than the type of control, because investment and other opportunities differ greatly among firms. One would ideally like to compare the actual retention policy in a firm with the policy that would maximize that firm's present value and then compare the magnitudes of these differences based on control type. But since the present-value-maximizing norm cannot be observed, contrasts among control types must suffice. Williamson in his analysis assumed that firms in the same industry have the same investment opportunities [139, p. 135]. This assumption will be borrowed for the present analysis, with industry dummy variables (D and L) included to account for any inter-industry differences in investment opportunities. Additional explanatory variables are included to account for differences in investment opportunities based on firm size and firm age. With control-type, industry-type, size, and age as explanatory variables, the expression is as follows:

$$Y_i = \varepsilon_0 + \varepsilon_1 OM + \varepsilon_2 MC + \varepsilon_3 D + \varepsilon_4 L + \varepsilon_5 S_i + \varepsilon_6 A_i + \mu_i \qquad (5.6)$$

where Y is the average payout ratio over the ten-year period 1963-1972.[f]

---

[f]This payout ratio was computed based on annual observations drawn from [93]. The figure for Clorox was computed during the period 1969-72.

OM and MC are control dummy variables (when OM and MC are both zero, the firm is externally-controlled), D and L are drug and petroleum industry dummy variables (when D and L are both zero the firm is in the chemical industry), S is a size variable and is measured by the firm's assets as of the end of 1972, and A is the firm's age. The only clear implication from the previous discussion concerning the control variables is that the OM group should have a higher fraction of retained profits than the EC group, and therefore will have a lower payout ratio ($\varepsilon_1 < 0$).

There is little than can be said a priori about how the preferences in MC firms compare with the other two groups. (Remember that any differences based solely on age should be picked up by the age variable.) Concerning the size variable a rather naive hypothesis follows if smaller firms have greater opportunities to expand and to invest, for they would presumably have greater need for retained earnings; that would mean that assets and the payout ratio should be positively related ($\varepsilon_5 > 0$). Likewise, Mueller's analysis [95] suggests that younger firms have greater need for capital so that the relationship between age and the payout ratio should be positive ($\varepsilon_6 > 0$). However, we must anticipate some multicollinearity problems since age is related to the control and industry terms and is also likely to be related to assets.

The results for the industry sample are as follows:

$$Y = \underset{(6.67)}{43.25} - \underset{(-3.56)}{18.97\text{OM}} + \underset{(0.83)}{3.33\text{MC}} - \underset{(-0.14)}{0.63\text{D}} - \underset{(-2.01)}{9.27\text{L}}$$
$$+ \underset{(1.62)}{0.001S} + \underset{(0.94)}{0.081A} \tag{5.7}$$

$R_a^2 = .40 \quad F = 6.15$

As predicted, the OM group has a significantly lower (at the 0.001 level) payout ratio than the EC group even after the effects of size and age are accounted for; an examination of the scatter diagram of residual terms suggests no problem with heteroscedasticity. There is no significant difference between the MC and EC firms, but the OM firms also pay out significantly less than the MC firms.[g] The petroleum industry has a significantly lower payout ratio than the chemical industry. The size and age

---
[g] By substituting an EC for an MC control dummy, the differences between the MC and OM groups can more easily be examined. This substitution is made in the following regression:

$$Y = \underset{(7.53)}{46.58} - \underset{(-4.42)}{22.30\text{OM}} - \underset{(-0.83)}{3.33\text{EC}} - \underset{(-0.14)}{0.63\text{D}} - \underset{(-2.01)}{9.27\text{L}}$$
$$+ \underset{(1.62)}{0.001S} + \underset{(0.94)}{0.081A} \tag{5.8}$$

The adjusted coefficient of determination and F-value remain the same as in (5.7)

variables have expected signs, but are not significant.[h]

One specific observation concerning retention policy in the externally-controlled firms is worth noting. Dupont, an externally-controlled firm, has ownership distributed over a large number of heirs. This was the only firm in the sample to reward the manager for dividends per se. The manager received "dividend units" based on the dividend-payout ratio. And Dupont had a higher payout ratio than any other firm in the sample.

The 96-firm sample that was described in Chapter 4, consisting of 32 firms in each of the three control types, was also used to test the effect of the control condition on retention policy. Because this sample was drawn at random from a number of industries, no means existed to account for inter-industry investment opportunities. Firm size was included as an explanatory variable because it proved significant in the industry sample when age was excluded. The Mueller-Grabowski analysis [97] found that dividends were paid to obtain security against a takeover, and those factors, such as a high rate of growth in earnings, which would keep stockholders happy and thereby diminish this threat were associated with lower payout ratios [97, p. 20]. In view of these findings the rate of return on stockholders' investment over the ten-year period was used as an additional explanatory variable as one measure of the manager's ability to retain earnings. The expression for the equation is as follows:

$$Y_i = \zeta_0 + \zeta_1 OM + \zeta_2 MC + \zeta_3 S_i + \zeta_4 G_i + \omega_i \tag{5.9}$$

where OM and MC are the owner-managed and manager-controlled dummy variables, S is the firm's assets, and G is the rate of return on a share purchased in December 1962 and held until December 1972.

Again the hypothesis concerning the control variable is that the OM group has a payout ratio lower than the EC group ($\zeta_1 < 0$). The hypothesis concerning the size variable remains the same; smaller firms have greater opportunities to expand and therefore have greater need for retained earnings ($\zeta_3 > 0$). And based on Mueller and Grabowski's findings, managers that produce higher rates of return on the stockholder's investment are more insulated from the market for corporate control, and are able to retain a larger fraction of earnings ($\zeta_4 < 0$). The results for the 96 firms are given in (5.10)

$$Y = 49.84 - 16.96 OM + 1.76 MC + 0.0018 S - 0.28 G \tag{5.10}$$
$$(14.04) \quad (-4.76) \quad (0.50) \quad (1.56) \quad (-1.94)$$

$R_a^2 = .34 \quad F = 13.26$

---

[h] Even though the simple correlation between the asset and age term is relatively small (r = .14), multicollinearity between these two variables probably reduced the significance levels of these two coefficients. When age is omitted from the regression, the asset term is positive and significant at the .05 level. When assets are omitted the age term increases in significance but is not significant at the .05 level.

The results in general are similar to the industry sample. The OM group again has a lower payout ratio than the EC group (ζ_1 is negative and significant at the 0.001 level). At the same time the EC and MC groups are not significantly different. Based on further analysis the MC group has a significantly higher payout ratio than the OM group.[i] The relationship between a firm's payout ratio and its combined rate of return over the ten-year period is negative and significant at the 0.05 level, supporting the earlier findings of Mueller and Grabowski [97]. We note also that the payout ratio appears to be inversely related to size, as expected, but this is not significant.

How do these results compare to previous work? Kamerschen [58] and Sorenson [126] grouped together owner-managed and externally-controlled firms and found that this single owner-controlled group had a significantly higher retention ratio than the manager-controlled group. Those results are consistent with the results here. If only the manager-controlled dummy variable is included, it is positive and significant for both the three-industry sample and the larger sample.[j] However, it is clear from our results that it is owner-managed firms, *not* externally-controlled firms, that differ in payout policy from management-controlled firms. At the same time neither earlier results nor our results should be interpreted as evidence that managers in manager-controlled firms retain less earnings than the average stockholder would prefer. Implications concerning the average stockholder's tastes simply cannot be applied to the dominant-stockholder firms.

An explanation of Williamson's results is a bit more involved. Recall that he used the internal composition of the board as his proxy for manage-

---

[i] After substituting an EC for an MC control dummy the results for the 96 firms are as follows:

$$Y = 51.60 - 18.72\text{OM} - 1.76\text{EC} + 0.0018S - 0.28G \quad (5.11)$$
$$(15.13) \quad (-5.05) \quad (-0.50) \quad (1.56) \quad (-1.94)$$

The adjusted coefficient of determination and F-value remain the same as in (5.10).

[j] The MC dummy variable is the only control variable included. The results for the three-industry 48-firm sample are as follows:

$$Y = 33.98 + 9.73\text{MC} - 0.67D - 10.07L + 12.60S - 0.12A \quad (5.12)$$
$$(5.06) \quad (2.39) \quad (-0.13) \quad (-1.94) \quad (1.82) \quad (-1.21)$$

$R_a^2 = .23 \quad F = 3.78$

where all variables are defined as in expression (5.6). The results for the large 96-firm sample are:

$$Y = 43.35 + 9.5\text{MC} - 0.40G + .002S \quad (5.13)$$
$$(11.39) \quad (2.71) \quad (-2.52) \quad (1.33)$$

$R_a^2 = 0.18 \quad F = 8.18$

where all variables are defined as in expression (5.9). In both regressions the MC group has a payout ratio that is about 9.5 percent higher than the owner-controlled group (both OM and EC). This difference is significant at the 0.025 level for the three-industry sample and the 0.005 level for the larger sample.

ment control and found that firms with a higher proportion of managers on the board retained a larger fraction of profits. Williamson admits that this fraction-of-managers-on-the-board variable is an unbiased estimate of the extent of management control only as long as it is not related to the actual distribution of control [139, p. 132]. But as shown in the previous chapter the fraction-of-managers-on-the-board was positively and significantly related to the presence of a dominant stockholder. Thus when Williamson speaks of "manager-controlled" firms he is very likely discussing firms with a dominant stockholder. As a check on Williamson's results the 96-firm sample was employed in a regression using the payout ratio as the dependent variable and an inside board[k] dummy variable, plus firm's asset and rate-of-return terms, as explanatory variables. The results were consistent with Williamson's findings indicating that firms with inside boards had significantly lower payout ratios. But when an owner-managed dummy variable was included in the regression as an additional explanatory variable, the inside board dummy was no longer significant, suggesting that the inside-board term had been serving in part as a proxy for owner-manager firms.[1] Thus Williamson's results are not inconsistent with anything found here, but more important they are not fully consistent with the theory of discretion that he was trying to test—namely that manager-controlled firms have a preference for retained earnings and this is reflected by a greater retention in firms with larger internal representations [137, pp. 134-39].

Two points should again be emphasized: the first is that dominant-stockholder firms should not be used to reflect the views of the average stockholder with respect to retention. Secondly, externally-controlled firms should not be coupled with owner-managed firms in examining issues involving managerial discretion.

---

[k] With inside boards a majority of the board of directors consists of managers. This was computed for each firm from the *Standard & Poor's Register of Corporations, Directors and Executives* [127].

[1] The regression for the sample of 96 firms with just the inside board is as follows:

$$Y = 49.95 - 6.17I + .002S - .46G \quad (5.14)$$
$$(14.07) \quad (-1.83) \quad (1.33) \quad (-3.02)$$

$R_a^2 = .15 \quad F = 6.60$

where I takes on the value of one when the managers represent a majority of the directors, S is firm assets, and G is the combined rate of return. The inside board term is significantly related to the payout ratio at the 0.05 level using a one-tailed test. When an owner-managed dummy variable is included the results are as follows:

$$Y = 52.11 - 3.96I - 17.19OM + .002S - 0.27G \quad (5.15)$$
$$(16.66) \quad (-1.33) \quad (-5.43) \quad (1.48) \quad (-1.96)$$

$R_a^2 = .35 \quad F = 13.86$

Note that the inside board dummy is no longer significant, but the owner-managed term is significant at the 0.001 level.

Risk and Control Type

Several studies were discussed in Chapter 3 which attempted to examine the contentions of Baumol [9, p. 103] and of Monsen and Downs [92, p. 225] that managers are less likely to take risks than owners because of asymmetry in the manager's income structure for reporting high and low profits, and because of the stockholders' remoteness from the day-to-day operations of the firm. Rather than maximize profits it is argued that managers aim at achieving a steady rate of growth in earnings and a gradual appreciation of the firm's market value. The results of three previous empirical studies were mixed. One found "owner-controlled" firms more risky [17]; another found "manager-controlled" firms more risky [101]; and a third was inconclusive [69]. Each used the two-class type-of-control approach, sorting firms into either owner-controlled or manager-controlled categories.

There appear to be two major problems, similar to those involved with the retention studies, associated with the theoretical and empirical work concerning risk based on the type of control, and these have led to confusion in formulating hypotheses concerning stockholders' and managers' attitudes toward risk. The first problem is that stockholders implicitly have been viewed as a homogeneous group with respect to their behavior concerning risk even though, as will be shown, there is reason to believe that dominant stockholders may view firm risk differently than will the average well diversified stockholder. Another problem with both the theoretical and empirical work is that it concentrated on only two categories of firms, even though the arguments presented imply behavior associated with three distinct groups. It will be shown, using in part the same arguments presented in earlier analyses, that if firms are to be sorted at all, the threefold classification system represents a more meaningful way of categorizing them and permits one to focus on the stockholders' and managers' incentive structures and consequent behavior concerning risk in each category.

Another problem that concerns previous empirical work is that the use of profit rate variability as a measure of risk yielded results that proved difficult to interpret. Since investors will want higher returns as they must bear more risk, there may be a link between profit rate variability and the level of profits. Boudreaux noted a link between profit rate variability and risk, but left it at that. Palmer attempted to integrate both risk and return with his coefficient of variation, but in doing so he implicitly specified an exact trade-off between risk and return that may or may not be the trade-off actually reflected in the market. It seems reasonable to assume, as did Palmer, that investors are more willing to tolerate larger standard deviations as long as higher profits are forthcoming, but it is another matter to assume that the coefficient of variation reflects precisely this trade-off.

In Part a the risks of stockholders and managers in each of the three control types will be examined. Based on this analysis, hypotheses concerning differences in risk based on control type will be stated and tested in Part b using two samples of large industrial firms. The final part will summarize the principle findings.

a. Manager and Stockholder Incentives

Previous analysis of risk based on control type implicitly assumed that stockholders were a homogeneous group. The typical stockholder is a diversified investor with a multi-firm viewpoint, but a dominant stockholder is likely to have a large portion of his portfolio tied up in one firm. The typical stockholder is more able to diversify his portfolio so that the risk associated with any single firm does not significantly affect the variability of his overall return. But the dominant stockholder is less able to diversify away the risk associated with the firm of which he owns a sizable fraction. If a firm in a well diversified portfolio fails, it is merely unfortunate for the stockholder, but if the firm held by a dominant stockholder goes bankrupt, it is likely to have a disastrous effect on his wealth position.[m] Since the dominant stockholder has a large fraction of his portfolio tied up in this one firm, he is consequently likely to be more averse to gambling with the performance of this particular firm than is the typical diversified investor. Therefore, when researchers use firms controlled by dominant stockholders as representative of the average stockholder's view towards risk they are apt to err, for as risk bearers (not to be confused with their role as entrepreneurs) dominant stockholders have greater reason to avoid risky actions than the average stockholder. And it seems inappropriate to draw inferences from these studies which compare the manager's risk preferences with the stockholder's risk preferences. It is one thing to say, based on empirical work of this sort, that managers usually follow policies that

---

[m] One might ask at this point why the dominant stockholder does not sell his shares, diversify his portfolio, and get some sleep. Well, many do; in Chapter 3 we considered a substantial body of literature indicating that dominant stockholders are becoming more scarce. But tax laws tend to have a lock-in effect. If he sells his shares (assuming he can do so without causing the market price to plummet), he must pay a capital-gain tax, but if he holds onto his shares, he can pass them to his heirs at death and escape the capital-gain tax entirely. A study of 47 major transactions involving the sale of 5 percent or more of the stock indicated that one of the primary reasons for stocks sales was to pay off estate taxes [31]; this suggests that owners were selling after a death in the family. Other reasons may account for maintaining a large fraction of the firm. He may have a more optimistic view of the firm's prospects than is expressed by the market. He may have founded the firm or may feel that he knows more about this firm than he does about any other potential investment. Or he may simply derive satisfaction from the attention accorded the dominant stockholder.

tend to be more or less conservative than those followed in firms with a dominant stockholder, but it is quite another thing to infer that these firms tend to be more or less conservative than the average stockholder would prefer. In reality, the manager and the dominant stockholder may view risk in the firm with similar attitudes—both have a large stake in the firm's survival.

Another problem with earlier empirical studies is that they coupled externally-controlled firms and owner-managed firms under the same heading of owner-controlled firms, even though the owners in the two cases are likely to view the firm from quite different perspectives. The owner-manager comes closest to our conception of the classical entrepreneur. He is likely to be more familiar with the day-to-day operations of the firm than is the outside owner, and he is more familiar with the extent and nature of the risks involved in following any particular course of action. Since the outsider is less intimately familiar with the daily machinations of the firm he may view with more alarm any unfamiliar variation in its performance. It is more difficult for the outsider to determine whether fluctuations in profits or market value are market-related or are more related to the manager's discretionary activity.[n] But he has a strong interest in finding out, and so the manager in the externally-controlled firm is in the most sensitive position of any manager; he most closely approximates the manager discussed by Baumol [9, p. 103] and Monsen and Downs [92, p. 224]. If this manager gambles for greater profits and fails, he is more apt to be replaced than is either the owner-manager or the manager in the manager-controlled firm.[o] The outside controller at best can lay down guidelines and evaluate the manager's overall performance, but he is not in a position to judge each decision, nor would this necessarily be wise since he is compensated only as a risk bearer, not as a manager. As a result of both the owner's remoteness from the day-to-day operations of the externally-controlled firm and his abiding great interest in results, the manager of an externally-controlled firm is likely to behave more conservatively than owner-managers or even managers in manager-controlled firms.

The owner-manager is the least constrained of managers in the three different control conditions. He has the widest range for discretion and he is not likely to be displaced even if some of his gambles fail. Robert Sheehan points out that the owner-manager is able to act quickly and boldly since he is not subject to the restraints of an overly cautious board; his actions often invite controversy and criticism which the professional manager might not risk [116, p. 82]. Thirty years ago Gordon argued: "[Owner-managers] are

---

[n] Monsen and Downs argue that since stockholders know less about the firm's operations, they are alarmed by erratic price movements even if the manager knows these movements are caused by forces which in the long run will increase the value of the stock [92, p. 225].

[o] Palmer made this same point [101, p. 228] but then proceeded to couple externally-controlled firms and owner-managed firms under his definition of owner-controlled firms.

more likely than professional executives to link their strategy directly to some concept of maximum profit for the firm, and they are also likely to pay more attention to short-period market changes" [48, p. 328]. At the same time, more than other managers, the owner-manager is in a position to capture the profits of a successful gamble. As Gordon noted: "The owner-enterpriser may be more willing to gamble his own money than the chief executive may be to jeopardize the financial empire of which he is trustee" [48, p. 322]. And again,

... more careful reckoning of probable costs and return lead the professional executive to reject investment possibilities that the old-fashioned entrepreneur might have accepted because of the possibilities of large gain if the venture succeeded at all. The profit-receiving entrepreneur is likely to overvalue small probabilities of large return [48, p. 330].

Another possible reason why owner-managed firms might tend to be more risky has been suggested by Alfred Chandler: "Strategies of diversification were rarely, if ever, carried out by . . . owner-executives. They were undertaken by professional managers (because of their education, background, and experience in managing large vertically integrated enterprises)" [22, p. 276]. Chandler's comments suggest that the owner-manager tended to stay in the product line which the family had always known; it was not until the leadership had passed to the hired manager that the firm began to diversify.

In sum the owner-manager has more incentive and more opportunity to take risks than the hired manager, but hired managers in externally-controlled firms are in the most sensitive position of all and are likely to be the most conservative of all. These propositions will be stated more explicitly and tested in the following section.

b. Testing for an Effect of Control Type on Risk

In testing for differences in risk based on the type of control, past procedure has been to employ some term related to the firm's year-to-year variability in profit rates [7, p. 367; 69, p. 31; 104, p. 229], but such a measure can be difficult to interpret since it may be related to the level of profitability. Rather than examine variability in profit rates, another approach to firm risk is to examine movements in the market value of the firm's share. In discussing risk Monsen and Downs argued that managers are concerned with the stability of share prices since ". . . up-and-down price movements create uncertainty in [the stockholder's] mind about the future price of the stock, thereby creating an apparent risk that he might suffer a loss if he had to sell at a certain moment" [92, p. 225]. Consequently, "the attention of management is focused on stock *prices* rather than *earnings* (profits)" [92, p. 233, italics in original].

One measure of share-price-related risk is the relationship between changes in the firm's share price and changes in the level of prices for the stock market as a whole. The less any one firm's share price responds to fluctuations in the stock market, the less risky that firm is, in part because the less the stockholder's "apparent risk that he might suffer a loss if he had to sell at a certain moment" [92, p. 225]. Gordon argued that ". . . conservation and careful planning should result in the professional business leader's avoiding some of the excesses of boom periods and should mitigate the effects of subsequent depressions" [48, p. 332]. Hence, conservatism should be reflected in a lower covariance between the firm's performance and swings in the market. Just such a covariance measure of risk called the "Beta coefficient" is well known in the financial literature.[p]

Our two samples were used to test for differences in this measure of firm risk based on type of control. First using the 48-firm industry sample, the firm's Beta coefficient was regressed on type of control and industry dummy variables as shown in (5.16)

$$\beta_i = \xi_0 + \xi_1 \text{OM} + \xi_2 \text{MC} + \xi_3 D + \xi_4 L + \xi_5 S_i + \mu_i \qquad (5.16)$$

where OM and EC are owner-managed and manager-controlled dummy variables; D and L are drug and petroleum industry dummies; and S is firm assets. Of primary interest here is the owner-managed dummy variable. The null hypothesis is that there is no difference in risk between EC and OM firms ($\xi_1 = 0$), against the one-sided alternative that OM firms are more risky ($\xi_1 > 0$).[q] The distinction between the EC and MC firm is less clear since there are professional managers in both cases. But without being as fully diversified in his investment, the external-controller is likely to be more averse to risk than the average stockholder, and the manager in the EC firm also is subject to more of a stockholder constraint than the manager in the MC firm, so we should predict that EC firms will tend to be more conservative than MC firms ($\xi_2 > 0$). The asset term is included to account for the possibility that larger firms tend to be more diverse and consequently may act more like a large sample of smaller firms. The expected

---

[p] To illustrate, a Beta coefficient of 1.5 indicates a stock tends to rise (or fall) 1.5 percent with a 1 percent rise (or fall) in the New York Stock Exchange Composite Average. One specific estimate of Beta coefficients is derived from least square regression analysis between the weekly percentage change in the price of each stock and the average weekly percentage change in the New York Stock Exchange Average over the five-year period 1968 through 1972 [134]. Although it is possible for the Beta coefficient to be negative, that is for a firm's share price to vary inversely with the stock market, such cases are unusual; there were no negative Beta coefficients in either of the samples used here.

[q] Note that the null hypothesis has been an implicit assumption in all previous empirical work on risk, since "owner-controlled" firms were viewed as a homogeneous group.

sign is therefore ($\xi_5 < 0$). The industry terms are included to account for inter-industry differences in risk.

The results for the industry sample consisting of 48 firms are as follows:

$$\begin{aligned}\beta = \;& 0.98 + 0.12\text{OM} + 0.06\text{MC} - 0.001\text{D} \\ & (20.07)\;(1.99) \quad\quad (1.40) \quad\quad (-0.025) \\ & + \;\; 0.056\text{L} - 0.000015S \\ & \quad\;\;(1.08) \quad\;\;\; (-2.16)\end{aligned} \quad (5.17)$$

$R_a^2 = .10 \quad F = 2.05$

The coefficients of the owner-managed dummy, OM, has the predicted sign and is significant at the 0.05 level.[r] The coefficient of the manager-controlled dummy also has the predicted sign but would be significant at only the 0.10 level. The asset term indicates that larger firms do have less market related risk. Neither of the industry terms is significant.

A sample of 96 firms, 32 of each control type, was also used to test these same hypotheses concerning risk. Since the industry terms were not significant in (5.17) there is more justification for using the larger sample without attempting to account for inter-industry differences. So the large sample was used with a test equation that included only the control dummy variables and the asset term. The results are:

$$\beta = 0.93 + 0.21\text{OM} + 0.17\text{MC} + 0.000001S \quad (5.18)$$
$$\quad\;(27.04)\;(4.61) \quad\;\;(3.68) \quad\quad (0.07)$$

$R_a^2 = .18 \quad F = 7.97$

where the variables are defined as in (5.16). Both the owner-manager and manager-controlled coefficients have the predicted positive sign, and both are significant at the 0.005 level.[s] The asset variable is no longer significant. In spite of the relatively large amount of risk that remains unexplained, we have grounds for concluding that there is more market-related risk in both the owner-managed firms and the manager-controlled firms than in externally-controlled firms. The owner-managed firms also appear to have a larger amount of market-related risk than the manager-controlled firms in both (5.17) and (5.18), but the difference is not significant.

Thus, in both the three-industry 48-firm sample and in the 96-firm

---

[r] Since Palmer's results suggest the possibility of a systematic relationship between size and risk, an interaction term for the asset and control variable was also included in the regressions for both the industry sample (5.17) and the large sample (5.18). But in neither case was the interaction term significant at even the 0.10 level.

[s] Of course there remains the possibility that some important variable was omitted. To the extent that any omitted variable is correlated with an included explanatory variable, the above results could be misleading. One such variable might be a measure for the firm's rate of return. As an additional check, the firm's combined rate of return was included as an additional explanatory variable in (5.18) but its inclusion did not affect the size or significance level of the type-of-control coefficients.

sample, there is a significant difference between externally-controlled and owner-managed firms, yet these two groups were thrown together in previous research. Moreover, rather than serving as a sharply different contrasting category the manager-controlled firms appear to fall *between* these two dominant stockholder groups, at least in terms of this measure of risk. Hence, any conclusions drawn from previous research about the manager's preference for risk versus the stockholder's are bound to be misleading. Even in the present study one cannot draw conclusions about the manager's versus the *average* stockholder's preference for risk. Failure to distinguish externally-controlled firms from owner-managed firms probably accounts for the significant—but opposite—results found by Boudreaux [17] and Palmer [101], as well as the inconclusive results found by Larner [69, p. 31], concerning the risk based on the type of control. Also, although Boudreaux and Palmer combined together externally-controlled and owner-managed firms into one group called "owner-controlled" firms, each researcher extracted different properties of the dominant-owner group to justify his results. Boudreaux, who found the dominant stockholder group to be significantly more risky than the manager-controlled group, compared the incentives facing the managers in his two groups by referring to the "different opportunity sets facing owner and non-owner managers" [17, p. 370]. Hence Boudreaux's view of the dominant stockholder group was in terms of the owner-manager's incentives. But Palmer, whose results showed the manager-controlled group was more risky, noted: ". . . it is the managers of *owner*-controlled corporations who must alter their behavior over time to keep the controlling stockholders happy" [101, pp. 228-229]. Thus he viewed the manager in the owner-controlled group as a hired manager, not an owner-manager. Obviously, they can't have both arguments accepted simultaneously. And if they focus on only one segment of the dominant-stockholder group in their interpretation they should also confine their sample to that segment.

One cannot necessarily conclude that firms have a lower market-related risk *because* they are externally-controlled. It may be that these firms remain externally-controlled *because* they have a lower market related risk. The dominant outside stockholders that had owned firms whose market value fluctuated more erratically may have decided long ago to diversify their portfolios. The phenomenon being observed here may be some sort of survival principle among firms that retain dominant outside stockholders—the survival of the safest.

Summary

After compensation structures had been examined in the previous chapter, the second section of this chapter attempted to evaluate the effectiveness of these incentives in influencing the performance of managers. The firm's combined rate of return (including dividends and capital gains) was the variable used to evaluate the manager's performance. The results indicated that both owner-managed and externally-controlled firms yielded significantly higher returns on a stockholder's investment than manager-controlled firms. The third and fourth sections considered two other aspects of firm performance based on the three categories of control: retention policy and firm risk. The results indicated that owner-managed firms retained more earnings and also exhibited a higher market-related risk than externally-controlled firms.

The main conclusion here is that the outside dominant stockholder views the firm primarily as an investment, while the owner-manager views it as a source of discretion as well, and is interested in all the pecuniary and nonpecuniary benefits that interest any manager. All previous research viewing retention and risk combined these two control groups under the heading of "owner-controlled" firms; it is no surprise that their results appear so confusing. When problems involving managerial discretion are examined in terms of three control categories rather than two, much of the previous confusion can be resolved.

6 Summary and Concluding Remarks

Although since the days of Adam Smith economists have been concerned with what has come to be known as the separation of ownership from control, the explicit formulations of alternative theories of the firm have appeared only in the past twenty years. In the first section of this chapter these alternative theories will be briefly summarized; in the second section the empirical work bearing on these theories will be reviewed, and the results of an alternative approach developed in this study to the issue of the separation of ownership from control will be summarized in the third section. Some concluding comments will be noted in the final section.

The Alternative Theories

Although the models of Baumol, Marris, Galbraith, and Williamson employed different assumptions, terminology, and constraints, they were shown to be more similar than they at first appear. All of the models concerned a large corporation which could be characterized as having separate ownership and control, and facing a downward sloping demand curve in its product market. The manager in each case was motivated by, among other things, his desire for income and security. In all cases income and security were linked to firm size. In each of the four models the manager tended to retain a larger fraction of earnings than would be required to maximize the value of the firm. Each theory posited an exogenously determined minimum performance constraint measured either in terms of profit or the firms' market value. By determining the minimum performance constraint exogenously, these theories begged the basic question of how much discretion the managers actually had and also ignored the possibility of interaction between the form of profit diversion by the manager and the profit constraint. The theories also implied irrational behavior on the part of managers who would join firms which, either because of stockholder control or product market constraints, afforded less room for managerial discretion. Why would a manager join this type of firm when he could join a firm that provided higher salaries, larger staff, more perquisites, and less pressure from product markets or stockholders?

After examining comparative static responses in output to changes in demand, a proportional tax and a lump-sum tax, it was noted that one could distinguish Baumol's sales-maximizing theory, Williamson's discretionary theory, or Leibenstein's X-theory from the neoclassical profit-maximization theory, but the alternative theories could not be distinguished from one another. Discriminating comparative dynamics were even more difficult to derive between the growth-maximizing theory and the long-run profit-maximization theory.

Previous Empirical Work

Past empirical work has examined the manager's incentives and constraints directly and has also viewed the consequences of the separation of ownership from control. We shall sketch empirical results under each category.

Managerial Incentives. At the beginning of the century executive compensation consisted primarily of salary that was unresponsive to year-to-year fluctuations in performance, but the fraction of the firm owned by the manager typically was higher then than it is today. Since then various forms of contingent and deferred compensation have become more prevalent, while the fraction of the firm held by top management has declined. Yet the value of executive holdings has remained large, and equity-related sources of income have actually become more important in the manager's total income, particularly since the 1950 legislation conveying favorable tax treatment to stock options. The early econometric research considering the relationship between compensation and both firm profitability and firm sales found that the manager's salary plus bonus was positively and significantly related to firm sales, but often unrelated to profits. More recent research, employing a more complete definition of income and adjusting for statistical problems encountered in the earlier studies, found on the contrary that executive incomes were positively and significantly related to profits and the firm's market value, but unrelated to sales. The two studies that attempted to look at differences in compensation based on the type of control were inconclusive, but problems were noted concerning the definition of control and the statistical procedures employed. The literature concerning the incentives for professional advancement through promotion examined primarily inter-firm executive mobility. There appeared to be little mobility among top executives, possibly suggesting that there was little inter-firm competition for promotion. Nothing could be said about the criteria applied to intra-firm competition for promotion.

Managerial Constraints. A look at the ownership of the large corporation indicated that the individual dominant stockholders are becoming rare.

Most studies concluded that control had passed to the management, but a few studies noted the increasing dominance of large financial institutions. Whether these institutions can exercise the control over management that was exercised by the dominant stockholder remains an unresolved issue. Thus far these institutions have shown little initiative in exercising control.

The empirical work concerning the market for corporate control suggests that such a market exists, but there is some question concerning its sensitivity or its overall impact in disciplining the manager. There were also problems found in testing for the sensitivity of this market since the more subtle the market actually is, the more difficult it becomes to observe differences between the firms that had been taken over and firms that had not been taken over.

Effects of the Separation of Ownership from Control. The studies which examined differences in firm performance based on the type of control divided firms into only two categories: (1) firms with a dominant stockholder (owner-controlled), and (2) firms without any controlling stockholder (manager-controlled). The studies focusing on firm profitability found with some consistency that owner-controlled firms provided higher average returns to shareholders than manager-controlled firms, but there was some question concerning the conclusions that could be drawn from this result. The examination of differences in firm risk based on control type showed that manager-controlled firms were significantly more risky or significantly less risky, depending on whose results were examined. Likewise, the examination of retained earnings found manager-controlled firms either retaining significantly more earnings or significantly less depending on the study. Two problems were noted in examining risk and retention based on the twofold classification of control. The first is that, primarily because of tax and portfolio effects, firms with a dominant stockholder should not be taken to reflect the tastes of the typical stockholder with respect to risk and retention, and secondly, firms in which the dominant stockholder is also the manager should not be coupled with firms in which the dominant stockholder is not part of management.

Two consistent findings of the previous empirical work were (1) that, particularly when considering the more recent studies, managers are paid to produce profit and market value, and (2) that firms with a dominant stockholding interest appear to have higher rates of return than manager-controlled firms. Yet these results, when viewed together, appear inconsistent; on the one hand the findings suggest that managers are paid to perform in the stockholders' interests, but on the other hand there is a difference in performance based on control type. If managers in general are paid for increases in profit and market value, then why the difference in performance?

An Alternative Approach

It was shown that if firms are to be sorted at all based on control categories, a sorting procedure which allows one to focus on the chief executive's incentives and constraints in each firm involves a threefold classification of firms including (1) firms with a dominant outside stockholder, (2) firms with a dominant stockholder acting also as manager, and (3) firms with no dominant stockholder. This classification system cleared up much of the confusion found in earlier research and more properly reflected the arguments implicit in the alternative theories of the firm.

After examining the manager's incentives and constraints under each of the three control conditions, several hypotheses were developed and tested concerning differences in management incentives and firm performance based on control. Nearly all of the discussion of the separation of ownership from control was in the context of the large industrial firm and our study focused on this population as well. The sample used to examine executive compensation consisted of sixteen large firms from each of three SIC three-digit industries that possessed large firms (drugs, chemicals, and petroleum). Data regarding executive compensation were collected from firm proxy statements during the period 1969-1972. Both before-tax salary-plus-bonus and full after-tax compensation were employed as definitions of compensation. This 48-firm industry sample together with a 96-firm sample made up of 32 firms drawn from each of three control categories were used to examine differences in various aspects of firm performance based on the firm's control condition.

Compensation Based on Control. Several hypotheses were developed and tested concerning not only differences in the compensation structure but differences in other performance characteristics based on the threefold classification of control. The results showed that the compensation structures of managers under the supervision of a dominant stockholder appeared to be more designed to maximize firm profits and market value than the compensation structure of managers in firms without a dominant stockholder. Firms with a dominant stockholder and a hired manager were paid more for profits and market value and less (penalized more) for sales, *ceteris paribus*, than managers in firms without a dominant stockholder. Also it appeared that the advantages of working in a firm free from the direction of a dominant stockholder were to some extent competed away, resulting in a lower level of compensation in those firms. The evidence concerning the compensation structure of firms with the dominant stockholder as manager was less clear, but their salary-plus-bonus structures appeared more similar to the structure in firms without a dominant stockholder than in firms with a dominant stockholder and a hired manager. Thus previous research that combined into one group firms with a dominant stockholder whether he served as manager or as outside controller mixed effects on compensation that could be traced to two distinctly different groups. However, when the fullest definition of compensation was employed the compensation structures in the owner-managed group appeared more like those in the externally-controlled group.

The impact of the industry type on the compensation structure was also examined. The hypothesis tested was that in an industry with a higher barrier to entry and hence greater market power, the managers could pay themselves more for size, making their salaries depend less on profit and market value. The analysis indicated that firms in the drug industry, which had higher barriers to entry than the other industries, were better able to make executive compensation depend more on sales and less on profit and market value. Moreover firms in the petroleum and chemical industries, industries which had the same barriers to entry, also had similar compensation structures. This inter-industry difference in compensation structure suggests that previous research on compensation which neglected industry effects may have left out some important information.

The tenure of the top executives also was examined based on the control situation. Tenure did not differ between firms with a dominant stockholder but a hired manager and firms without any dominant stockholder, but the dominant stockholders who also served as managers had average tenures about twice as long as managers in the other two control types.

Other Effects Based on Control. After examining the manager's positive and negative incentive the next step was to evaluate the effectiveness of these incentives on the returns to stockholders. The firm's combined rate of return (including dividend and capital gains) over a ten-year period was the variable used to evaluate the manager's performance. The results indicated that both dominant stockholder firms with hired managers and dominant stockholder firms with owner-managers yielded significantly higher rates of return on a stockholder's investment than firms without a dominant stockholder. An examination of firm retention policies indicated, as predicted, that firms with the dominant stockholder as manager retained significantly more earnings than firms with a dominant stockholder not part of management. The outside dominant stockholder viewed the firm primarily as an investment, while the owner-manager viewed it not only as an investment but as a source of discretion. The owner-manager was interested in all the pecuniary and nonpecuniary benefits that would interest any manager. Owner-managed firms were also more risky than externally-controlled firms. The owner-manager had more incentive and more opportunity to take risks than the manager controlled by an outside dominant stockholder. Previous research combined owner-managed firms with externally-controlled firms and compared this combination to firms without a dominant stockholder. It is no wonder that the results derived from these studies appear so confusing. When issues involving managerial discretion were examined in terms of three control categories rather than two, much of the previous confusion was resolved.

Conclusions

Owner-managers tend to conform to the image of the risk-taking, empire-building, classical entrepreneur. When the owner hires the chief executive, rather than manage the firm himself, the firm appears to be less risky and retain a smaller fraction of earnings. But whether the owner runs the firm himself or hires the manager, the evidence appears strong that firms which still have a dominant stockholder produce a higher rate of return for stockholders than do firms without a dominant stockholder. This study has shown that this higher return can be traced to the compensation structure which the managers in those firms face. Moreover, our analysis was largely free of the identification problem caused by the natural link between equity-related income and firm performance. An examination of other issues raised by alternative theories of the firm such as executive tenure, firm risk, and firm retention policy based on type of control found significant differences between two groups that had been viewed as homogeneous in all previous empirical work. The threefold classification of control proved to be a more fertile and less ambiguous way of sorting firms than the previously used twofold classification system.

Appendixes

Appendix A
Owner-Manager's Incentive Structure

Assume the owner-manager faces the choice of taking one dollar in salary or leaving it in the firm and claiming it as dividends or capital gains. If he takes it as salary his after-tax return in $1 - T_p$ where T_p is the personal tax rate. However, if he leaves it as reported profits, and receives it as dividends and capital gains his after-tax share is

$$m[(1 - T_p)d + (1 - T_g)(1 - d)](1 - T_c)$$

where m is his fraction of the firm, T_p is the personal tax rate, T_g is the capital-gain tax rate, T_c is the corporate income tax rate, and d is the dividend-payout ratio. Assume for simplicity that if profits are retained by the firm they earn a return equal to the owner-manager's rate of time preference. For the dollar in salary to be preferred to his share of the profit stream then the following must hold:

$$1 - T_p > m[(1 - T_p)d + (1 + T_g)(1 - d)](1 - T_c).$$

Two reasonable simplifying assumptions will permit more specific conclusions. Assume the corporate tax rate is 50 percent and the capital-gain tax rate is 25 percent. The expression then becomes

$$(1 - T_p) > m[(1 - T_p)d + (3/4)(1 - d)]\,1/2.$$

After manipulating terms the expression reduces to

$$\frac{8 - md - 3m}{8 - 4md} > T_p.$$

Thus the dollar will be taken in salary as long as the left-hand expression is greater than the personal tax rate. Salary is least attractive when he is the sole owner ($m = 1$) and all profits are retained ($d = 0$) and are thereby subjected to the more favorable capital-gain tax. In this case the expression reduces to $5/8 > T_p$, so if the personal income tax is less than 62.5 percent, the owner prefers salary to profits. If the fraction of the firm held by the owner is lower, or if the dividend payout ratio is greater, salary becomes even more attractive. For example, if the manager owns half the firm ($m = 1/2$) and the firm pays out half the profits in dividends ($d = 1/2$), then the owner-manager prefers his income in salary if his personal tax rate is less than 89.3 percent.

This holds as long as we assume that the owner-manager is the only executive or that the salary received by other executives in the firm is independent of the owner-manager's salary. But empirical work suggests that executive salaries are carefully scaled and are therefore highly correlated among executive levels [25; 70; 119]. Therefore assume that when the top executive's salary changes all other salaries change proportionately. Assume the owner-manager's salary represents a constant fraction, c, of the total wage bill for all executives. So if the owner-manager increases his salary by one dollar, this costs him

$$\frac{m[(1 - T_p)d + (1 - T_g)(1 - d)](1 - T_c)}{c}$$

in his share of foregone profits. A dollar in additional salary will now be preferred to the owner-manager's share of profits as long as

$$(1 - T_p) > \frac{m[(1 - T_p)d + (1 - T_g)(1 - d)](1 - T_c)}{c},$$

which reduces to

$$\frac{8c - 3m - md}{8c - 4md} > T_p.$$

Now, when $m = 1$ and $d = 0$, the expression reduces to

$$\frac{8c - 3}{8c} > T_p.$$

If the owner-manager receives the entire executive wage bill ($c = 1$) then the above expression reduces to $5/8 > T_p$, which is what was derived earlier, but as c grows smaller, the left-hand expression also grows smaller and salary becomes less attractive; if c drops below 0.375 the left-hand expression becomes negative and additional salary will never be preferred under the $m = 1$, $d = 0$ assumptions. Of course if m is lowered or d is raised the salary route again becomes more attractive.

Appendix B
Calculation of Executive Compensation

In general Wilbur Lewellen's procedure [70] was followed in computing the after-tax value of executive compensation. But our time frame was four years whereas Lewellen's was twenty-four; consequently some differences appear in the derivation procedure and these differences will be noted. The tax rates used were those in effect for each year as a result of the Tax Reform Act of 1969 [106]. Like Lewellen we assumed that each executive was able to deduct 15 percent of his income. Procedures involved in calculating each specific form of compensation are briefly summarized in the following sections.

Stock Options

An *ex post* value of stock options was calculated in the following manner. If the option was exercised, the option price was subtracted from the share price at which the option was exercised. If the option was still unexercised at the end of 1972, and the closing price of the share on the last trading day of the year exceeded the option price, it was assumed that the option had been exercised on that day and its return was computed as above. If the closing price was less than or equal to the option price, the option was assigned a value of zero. Admittedly, an *ex ante* measure of stock options reflecting the discounted prospective gains from exercising the option would have been a superior measure, but the practical difficulties of deriving such a measure proved insurmountable. The options issued to executives are transferable only at death and only to their heirs, so there is no established market to determine their value.

Executives had after-tax incomes large enough to be subject to the maximum capital-gain tax rate. Based on the Tax Reform Act of 1969 the maximum capital-gain tax rate went from 25 percent in 1969 to 35 percent in 1972; this increase was accounted for in our analysis. Lewellen points out three reasons why the capital-gain tax rate the executive actually pays might be lower than the maximum rate. The first is that the executive can pass his stock to his heirs at death and avoid the tax altogether. The second is that the executive may borrow to purchase the optioned shares and thereby he incurs deductible interest. Finally, the executive may be induced to increase his charitable contributions as a result of his increased tax liability [70, p. 53]. Lewellen admits that there is no way of knowing the quantitative impact of these phenomena yet he reduces the actual capital-gain tax rate by a total of 10 percent as a result, noting "While arbitrary—and quite unverifiable—the resulting adjustment does at least operate to change the imputed tax liabilities in the proper direction" [70, p. 53]. Lewellen's procedure was adopted in this study.

Pension Plans

The value of an executive's pension was taken to be the stream of annual premiums which—given an after-tax salary increase of the same amount—would enable the executive to purchase an individual retirement annuity having a present value equal to that of the pension. Premium rates were based on the average quoted rates for two major insurance companies (Connecticut General Life Insurance Company and The Travelers Insurance Company) for a comparable annuity plan.[a] Since knowledge of the executive's pension plan prior to 1969 was unknown, it was assumed that the pension plan in effect in 1969 had been in effect for five years. The value of pension plans depends primarily on the age of the executive. The closer the executive is to sixty-five (which, as with Lewellen, was assumed to be retirement age), the more highly valued a given increase in retirement benefits becomes.

Deferred Compensation

The executive is often promised a series of cash payments after retirement in return for services performed currently, subject to certain contingencies. Such contingencies include staying with the firm until retirement, promising not to divulge any inside information concerning the firm's operation, and/or serving as a consultant after retirement. Lewellen argues that because the executive has so much to lose, these payments may be viewed as certain insofar as the executive's part of the agreement goes [70, p. 42].[b] Our analysis also assumes that this sort of contingency is certain. Deferred compensation was discounted at 5 percent.[c] In our sample deferred compensation represented a relatively small fraction of total income.

---

[a] These average rates appear in Lewellen's Appendix K [70, pp. 337-38].

[b] One might argue that at least part of the payment received by the retired executive should be regarded as remuneration for services he is performing at that time. But Lewellen follows the view that "the timing of such payments is simply a matter of compensation administration and tax planning, and that the rewards really apply to the man's active working life" [70, p. 39]. Lewellen contends that "consulting chores, are, in practice, almost invariably quite nominal and hardly represent a realistic quid pro quo for the payments he is receiving" [70, p. 39].

[c] As noted earlier the choice of a discount rate could introduce a bias to the extent that the age of executives differed across control type, but a check found no significant differences in the age of executives based on control type.

Contributions to Savings Plans

Some firms contributed to a savings plan in the name of the executive. A simplifying assumption was made here: it was assumed that these savings grew at a rate of 5 percent, so given the discount rate of 5 percent, contributions to savings plans were valued at their actual amounts. These represented a relatively small fraction of compensation. Lewellen ignored contributions to savings plans.

Not Considered

Certain items had to be excluded because of lack of information concerning individual executives. These were the benefits received from life and medical insurance programs, expense account provisions, plus any payment in kind. To the extent that these forms of compensation differed systematically across control types, such exclusion could bias the results. Lewellen also ignored these forms of compensation.

Appendix C
The Sample

Table C-1
Industry Sample

Chemical Firms	*Drug Firms*
Airco (MC)	Abbot Laboratories (MC)
Air Products & Chemicals (OM)	American Home Products (MC)
Akzona (MC)	Baxter Laboratories (OM)
Allied Chemical (MC)	Bristol-Myers (MC)
American Cyanamid (MC)	Carter-Wallace (EC)
Celanese (MC)	Eil Lilly (EC)
Clorox (MC)	Merck (EC)
Diamond Shamrock (MC)	Miles (EC)
Dow Chemical (EC)	Pfizer (MC)
E.I. duPont (EC)	Richardson-Merrell (MC)
W.R. Grace (MC)	A.H. Robins (OM)
Hercules (MC)	Searle (OM)
International F & F (OM)	Smith Kline Corporation (EC)
Monsanto (MC)	Sterling Drug (MC)
Rohm & Haas (EC)	Upjohn (EC)
Stauffer Chemical (MC)	Warner-Lambert (MC)

Petroleum Refining Firms

Amerada Hess (OM)
Ashland Oil (MC)
Atlantic Richfield (MC)
Cities Service (MC)
Clark Oil (EC)
Continental Oil (MC)
Getty Oil (OM)
Gulf Oil (EC)
Kerr-McGee (OM)
Marathon Oil (MC)
Mobil Oil (MC)
Phillips Petroleum (MC)
Quaker State Oil (EC)
Shell Oil (EC)
Standard Oil of N.J. (MC)
Sun Oil (EC)

Table C-2
Large Sample

Manager-Controlled Firms	Owner-Managed Firms	Externally-Controlled Firms
Abbot Laboratories	Air Products & Chemicals	Alcoa
ABC	Amerada Hess	American Metal Climax
Allegheny-Ludlum	American Greetings	Anderson-Clayton
Allied Chemical	Anheuser-Busch	Campbell Soup
Allis-Chalmers	CBS	Carnation
American Cyanamid	Champion Spark Plugs	Coca-Cola
American Home Products	Corning Glass	Consolidated Foods
American Motors	Crane	Dana
Anaconda	Cummins Engine	E.I. duPont
Anchor-Hocking	Deere	Hoover
Armco Steel	Digital Equipment	H.J. Heinz
Ashland	Electronic Data	Hershey Foods
Avco	Ethyl	Interlake Iron
Babcock & Wilcox	Firestone	Eli Lilly
Bendix	Ford	Lowenstein
Bethlehem Steel	General Tire	McGraw-Hill
Boeing	Getty Oil	Merck
Bordon	Hewlett-Packard	National Steel
Borg Warner	International F & F	Norton
Bristol-Myers	Kerr-McGee	Pet Foods
Burlington	Loews	Quaker State Oil
Burroughs	MCA	Ralston Purina
Carrier	McDonald-Douglas	Rohm & Haas
Celanese	Motorola	Shell Oil
Cerro	Polaroid	Signal Oil
Charles Pfizer	Revlon	Singer
Crysler	A.H. Robins	SmithKline
Clark Equipment	Schlitz	Sun Oil
Colgate-Palmolive	Searle	Time
Combustion Engineering	Skyline Corporation	Timken
Continental Can	A.O. Smith	Upjohn
Continental Oil	Williams Company	3M

Bibliography

1. Alchian, Armen A. "Corporate Management and Property Rights." In *Economic Policy and the Regulation of Corporate Securities*, pp. 337-60. Edited by Henry G. Manne. Washington, D.C.: American Enterprise Institute, 1969.
2. _____. "The Basis of Some Recent Advances of Management of the Firm." *Journal of Industrial Economics* 14 (November 1965): 130-41.
3. _____. "Uncertainty, Evolution, and Economic Theory." *Journal of Political Economy* 58 (June 1950): 211-21.
4. _____, and Kessel, Reuben A. "Competition, Monopoly, and the Pursuit of Pecuniary Gain." In *Aspects of Labor Economics*. Edited by Universities-National Bureau Committee for Economic Research. Princeton University Press, 1962.
5. Baker, John Calhoun. *Executive Salaries and Bonus Plans*. New York: McGraw-Hill, 1938.
6. _____. "Stock Options for Executives." *Harvard Business Review* 19 (Autumn 1940): 106-22.
7. Baker, S.H. "Executive Incomes, Profits, and Revenues: A Comment on Functional Specification." *Southern Economic Journal* 25 (April 1969): 379-83.
8. Baumol, William. *Business Behavior, Value and Growth*. New York: The Macmillan Company, 1959.
9. _____. *Business Behavior, Value and Growth*. rev. ed. New York: Harcourt, Brace & World, Inc., 1967.
10. _____. *The Stock Market and Economic Efficiency*. New York: Fordham University Press, 1965.
11. Beard, Miriam. *A History of the Business Man*. New York: The Macmillan Company, 1938.
12. Becker, Gary S. "Irrational Behavior and Economic Theory." *Journal of Political Economy* 70 (February 1962): 1-13.
13. Berle, Adolf A. *Power Without Property*. New York: Harcourt, Brace & World, Inc., 1959.
14. _____ et al. "Symposium on the Impact of the Corporation on Classical Economic Theory." *Quarterly Journal of Economics* 79 (February 1965): 1-51.
15. _____, and Means, Gardiner C. *The Modern Corporation and Private Property*. rev. ed. New York: Harcourt, Brace & World, 1968.
16. "Big-Block Buyers May Speak Up." *Business Week*, November 26, 1966, pp. 139-40.

17. Boudreaux, Kenneth J. "Managerialism and Risk-Return Performance." *Southern Economic Journal* 39 (January 1973): 366-73.
18. Bower, Richard S. "Managerialism and the Risk-Return Performance: Comment." *Southern Economic Journal* 40 (January 1974): 505-506.
19. Boyle, Stanley E. and Hogarty, Thomas F. "'Good' News v. 'Bad' News: Another Aspect of the Controversy between Manager and Owner." *Industrial Organization Review* 1 (November 1973): 1-14.
20. Buchanan, Norman S. "Theory and Practice in Dividend Distribution." *Quarterly Journal of Economics* 53 (November 1938): 64-85.
21. Burch, Philip H., Jr. *The Managerial Revolution Reassessed*. Lexington, Massachusetts: Lexington Books, D.C. Heath and Company, 1972.
22. Chandler, Alfred D., Jr. *Strategy and Structure: Chapters in the History of the American Industrial Enterprise*. Boston: Massachusetts Institute of Technology Press, 1969.
23. Chevalier, Jean-Marie. "The Problem of Control in Large American Corporations." *Antitrust Bulletin* 14 (Spring 1969): 163-80.
24. Ciscel, David H. "Determinants of Executive Compensation." *Southern Economic Journal* 40 (April 1974): 613-17.
25. The Conference Board. *Top Executive Compensation*, New York: The Conference Board, Inc., 1970.
26. Cox, Edwin B. *Trends in the Distribution of Stock Ownership*. Philadelphia: University of Pennsylvania Press, 1963.
27. Crew, M.A.; Jones-Lee, M.W.; and Rowley, C.K. "X-Theory Versus Management Discretion Theory." *Southern Economic Journal* 38 (October 1971): 173-84.
28. Crum, W.L. "Analysis of Stock Ownership." *Harvard Business Review* 20 (May-June 1953): 36-54.
29. Cyert, R.M. and March, J.G. *A Behavioral Theory of the Firm*. Englewood Cliffs, N.J.: Prentice-Hall, Inc., 1963.
30. Dale, Ernest. "Management Must Be Made Accountable." *Harvard Business Review* 38 (May-June 1960): 49-59.
31. Dauten, Joel J. "The Economic Impact and Significance of Substantial Stock Sales by Individual Stockholders." Ph.D. dissertation, State University of Iowa, 1954.
32. DeAlessi, Louis. "Managerial Tenure under Private and Government Ownership in the Electric Power Industry." *Journal of Political Economy* 82 (May/June 1974): 645-53.
33. _____. "Private Property and Dispersion of Ownership in Large Corporations." *Journal of Finance* 28 (September 1973): 839-51.

34. Donaldson, Gordon. *Corporate Debt Capacity*. Boston: Harvard University Press, 1961.
35. Dooley, P.C. "The Interlocking Directorate." *American Economic Review* 59 (June 1969): 314-23.
36. Durbrow, Brian R. "Inter-Firm Executive Mobility: An Empirical Study of Relationships, Comparisons, and Patterns." Ph.D. dissertation, Ohio State University, 1971.
37. Editors of *News Front, 25,000 Leading U.S. Corporations*. New York: News Front, 1970.
38. Fama, E.F. and Miller, M.H. *The Theory of Finance*. New York: Holt, Rinehart and Winston, 1972.
39. "The *Forbes* Five Hundreds." *Forbes*, May 15, 1970-73.
40. "*Fortune* Annual Directory of Corporations." *Fortune*. May and June, 1970-73.
41. Friedman, Milton. *Essays in Positive Economics*. Chicago: University of Chicago Press, 1953.
42. Furubotn, Eirik and Pejovich, Svetozar. "Property Rights and Economic Theory: A Survey of Recent Literature." *Journal of Economic Literature* 10 (December 1972): 1137-62.
43. Galbraith, John Kenneth. *Economics and the Public Purpose*. Boston: Houghton Mifflin Company, 1973.
44. _____. *The New Industrial State*. Boston: Houghton Mifflin Company, 1967.
45. _____. "A Review of a Review." *The Public Interest* (Fall 1967): 109-15.
46. "Going After the Banks." *The New Republic*, July 20, 1968, pp. 13-14.
47. Gordon, Myron J. *The Investment Financing and Valuation of the Corporation*. Homewood Ill.: R.D. Irwin, 1962.
48. Gordon, Robert A. *Business Leadership in the Large Corporation*. Berkeley: University of California Press, 1961.
49. Hald, A. *Statistical Tables and Formulas*. New York: John Wiley & Sons, Inc., 1952.
50. Hall, M. and Weiss, L. "Firm Size and Profitability." *Review of Economics and Statistics* 49 (August 1967): 319-31.
51. Hayes, Samuel L. and Taussig, Russell A. "Tactics of Cash Takeover Bids." *Harvard Business Review* 45 (March-April 1967): 135-48.
52. Hicks, John R. "Survey of the Theory of Monopoly." *Econometrica* 3 (January 1935): 1-20.
53. Higgins, Benjamin. "Indeterminancy in Non-Perfect Competition." *American Economic Review* 29 (September 1939): 468-79.

54. Hindley, Brian. "Capitalism and the Corporation." *Economica* 32 (November 1969): 426-38.
55. _____. "Separation of Ownership and Control in the Modern Corporation." *Journal of Law and Economics* 13 (April 1970): 185-221.
56. Johnston, John. *Econometric Methods*. 2nd ed., New York: McGraw-Hill, 1972.
57. Jorgensen, Leon P. "Separation of Ownership and Control and Its Influence on the Profit Performance of the Large Firm." Ph.D. dissertation, Florida State University, 1972.
58. Kamerschen, David R. "A Theory of Conglomerate Mergers: Comment." *Quarterly Journal of Economics* 84 (November 1970): 668-73.
59. _____. "The Effect of Separation of Ownership and Control on the Performance of the Large Firm in the U.S. Economy." *Revisita Internazionale Di Scienze Economiche e Commerciali* 15 (July 1969): 293-301.
60. _____. "The Influence of Ownership and Control on Profit Rates." *American Economic Review* 63 (June 1968): 432-47.
61. Karst, Philip J. "The Effect on Performance of the Separation of Ownership from Control." Ph.D. dissertation, Washington University, 1972.
62. Keynes, John Maynard. *Essays in Persuasion*. London: Macmillan & Company, Ltd., 1931.
63. Kmenta, J. *Elements of Econometrics*. New York: Macmillan, 1971.
64. Knight, Frank H. *Risk, Uncertainty and Profit*. Boston and New York: Houghton Mifflin Company, 1921.
65. Knowles, James C. *The Rockefeller Financial Group*. Andover, Massachusetts: Warner Modular Publications, 1973.
66. Koch, James V. *Industrial Organization and Prices*. Englewood Cliffs N.J.: Prentice-Hall, Inc., 1974.
67. Kolko, Gabriel. *Wealth and Power in America*. New York: Frederick A. Praeger, Inc., 1962.
68. Kuehn, D.A. "Stock Market Valuations and Acquisitions: An Empirical Test of a Component of Managerial Utility." *Journal of Industrial Economics* 17 (April 1969): 132-44.
69. Larner, Robert J. *Management Control and the Large Corporation*. New York: Dunellen Publishing Company, 1970.
70. Lewellen, Wilbur G. *Executive Compensation in Large Industrial Corporations*. New York: National Bureau of Economic Research, 1968.
71. _____. "Managerial Pay and the Tax Changes of the 1960's." *National Tax Journal* 25 (June 1972): 111-31.

72. _____. *The Ownership Income of Management*. New York: National Bureau of Economic Research, 1971.
73. _____, and Huntsman, Blaine. "Managerial Pay and Corporate Performance." *American Economic Review* 60 (September 1970): 710-20.
74. Leibenstein, Harvey. "Allocative Efficiency vs. X-Efficiency." *American Economic Review* 56 (June 1966): 342-415.
75. _____. "Organizational or Frictional Equilibrium, X-Efficiency, and the Rate of Innovation." *Quarterly Journal of Economics* 83 (November 1969): 600-23.
76. Lintner, John. "The Financing of Corporations." *The Corporation in Modern Society*, pp. 166-201. Edited by Edward S. Mason. Cambridge: Harvard University Press, 1960.
77. Lipsey, Richard G. and Steiner, Peter O. *Economics*. 3rd. ed. New York: Harper and Row, 1972.
78. Mann, H. Michael. "Seller Concentration, Barriers to Entry, and Rates of Return in Thirty Industries, 1950-1960." *Review of Economics and Statistics* 48 (August 1966): 295-307.
79. Manne, Henry G. *Insider Trading and the Stock Market*. New York: The Free Press, 1966.
80. _____. "Mergers and the Market for Corporate Control." *Journal of Political Economy* 73 (April 1965): 110-20.
81. _____. "Our Two Corporation Systems: Law and Economics." *Virginia Law Review* 53 (March 1967): 259-84.
82. _____. "Some Theoretical Aspects of Share Voting." *Columbia Law Review* 69 (March 1964): 1427-48.
83. Marris, Robin. *The Economic Theory of 'Managerial' Capitalism*. London: Macmillan, 1967.
84. _____. "Galbraith, Solow, and the Truth About Corporations." *The Public Interest* 11 (Spring 1969): 37-46.
85. Marshall, Alfred. *Industry and Trade*. London: The Macmillan Company, 1932.
86. Masson, Robert Tempest. "Executive Motivations, Earnings, and Consequent Equity Performance." *Journal of Political Economy* 79 (November/December 1971): 1278-92.
87. McEachern, William A. "Stockholder Voting and Corporate Control." Master's thesis, Department of Economics, University of Virginia, 1969.
88. McGuire, J.W.; Chiu, J.S.Y.; and Elbing, A.O. "Executive Incomes, Sales and Profits." *American Economic Review* 52 (September 1962): 753-61.

89. Meade, J.E. "Is 'The New Industrial State' Inevitable?" *Economic Journal* 78 (June 1968): 372-92.
90. Monsen, R.J.; Chiu, J.S.Y.; and Cooley, D.E. "The Effect of Separation of Ownership and Control on the Performance of the Large Firm." *Quarterly Journal of Economics* 83 (August 1968): 435-51.
91. _____ et al. Unpublished Appendix to "The Effect of the Separation of Ownership and Control on the Performance of the Large Firm." *Quarterly Journal of Economics* 82 (August 1968): 435-51. (Mimeographed.)
92. _____, and Downs, A. "A Theory of Large Managerial Firms." *Journal of Political Economy* 73 (June 1965): 221-36.
93. *Moody's Handbook of Common Stocks*. New York: Moody's Investors Service, Inc., 1973.
94. *Moody's Industrial Manual*. New York: Moody's Investors Service, 1952-63.
95. Mueller, Dennis C. "A Life Cycle Theory of the Firm." *Journal of Industrial Economics* 20 (July 1972): 192-219.
96. _____. "A Theory of Conglomerate Mergers: Reply." *Quarterly Journal of Economics* 84 (November 1970): 675-79.
97. _____, and Grabowski, Henry G. "Managerial and Stockholder Welfare Models of Firm Expenditures." *Review of Economics and Statistics* 54 (February 1972): 9-24.
98. Nicholson, Walter. *Microeconomic Theory*. Hinsdale, Ill.: The Dryden Press, Inc., 1972.
99. Noether, Gottfried. *Introduction to Statistics*. Boston: Houghton Mifflin Company, 1971.
100. Papandreou, A.G. "Some Basic Issues in the Theory of the Firm." In *A Survey of Contemporary Economics*. Edited by B.F. Haley. Homewood, Ill.: Richard D. Irwin, Inc., 1952.
101. Palmer, John. "The Profit Variability Effects of the Managerial Enterprise." *Western Economic Journal* 11 (June 1973): 228-31.
102. _____. "A Further Analysis of Profit Variability and Managerialism." *Economic Inquiry* 12 (March 1975): 127-29.
103. _____. "The Profit Performance Effects of the Separation of Ownership from Control in Large U.S. Industrial Corporations." *The Bell Journal of Economics and Management Science* 3 (Spring 1973): 293-303.
104. _____. Unpublished Appendix to "The Profit Performance Effects of the Separation of Ownership from Control in Large U.S. Industrial Corporations." *The Bell Journal of Economics and Management Science* 3 (Spring 1973): 293-303.

105. _____. "The Separation of Ownership from Control in Large U.S. Industrial Corporations." *Quarterly Review of Economics and Business* 12 (Autumn 1972): 55-62.
106. Pechman, Joseph A. *Federal Tax Policy*. rev. ed. Washington: The Brookings Institution, 1971.
107. Penrose, Edith. *The Theory of the Growth of the Firm*. New York: Wiley, 1959.
108. Radice, H.K. "Control Type, Profitability and Growth in Large Firms: An Empirical Study." *The Economic Journal* 81 (September 1971): 547-62.
109. Roberts, David R. *Executive Compensation*. Glencoe Ill.: The Free Press, 1959.
110. A.H. Robins Company. *Annual Proxy Statement*. March 1972.
111. Rostow, E.V. "To Whom and for What Ends Is Corporate Management Responsible?" *The Corporation in Modern Society*, pp. 46-71. Edited by Edward S. Mason. Cambridge: Harvard University Press, 1959.
112. Scherer, F.M. *Industrial Market Structure and Economic Performance*. Chicago: Rand McNally & Company, 1970.
113. Schumpeter, Joseph A. *The Theory of Economic Development*. Cambridge: Harvard University Press, 1934.
114. Scitovski, Tibor. "A Note on Profit Maximization and Its Implications." *Review of Economic Studies* 11 (1943): 57-60.
115. Securities and Exchange Commission. *Directory of Companies*. Washington, D.C.: U.S. Government Printing Office, 1972.
116. Sheehan, Robert. "Proprietors in the World of Big Business." *Fortune*, June 1967, pp. 178-83.
117. Shepherd, William G. *Market Power & Economic Welfare*. New York: Random House, 1970.
118. Sherman, Roger. *The Economics of Industry*. Boston: Little, Brown and Company, 1974.
119. Simon, Herbert A. "The Compensation of Executives." *Sociometry* 20 (March 1957): 32-35.
120. _____. "Theories of Decision Making in Economics and Behavioral Science." *American Economic Review* 49 (June 1959): 253-83.
121. Singh, Agit. *Take-overs: Their Relevance to the Stock Market and the Theory of the Firm*. Cambridge: The University Press, 1971
122. Smith, Adam. *An Inquiry into the Nature and Causes of the Wealth of Nations*. Edited by Edward Cannan. New York: Modern Library, Inc., 1937.

123. Solow, Robert. "Some Implications of Alternative Criteria for the Firm." In *The Corporate Economy*. Edited by Robin Marris and Adrian Wood. Cambridge: Harvard University Press, 1971.
124. _____. "The New Industrial State or Son of Affluence." *The Public Interest* (Fall 1967): 100-108.
125. Sorenson, Robert L. "Some Economic Implications of the Separation of Ownership and Control in the Large Firm." Ph.D. dissertation, Virginia Polytechnic Institute and State University, 1971.
126. _____. "The Separation of Ownership and Control and Firm Performance; An Empirical Analysis." *Southern Economic Journal* (July 1974): 145-48.
127. *Standard & Poor's Register of Corporations, Directors and Executives*. New York: Standard & Poor's Corporation, 1972.
128. Stigler, George J. *The Theory of Price*. 3rd ed. New York: The Macmillan Company, 1966.
129. Sweezy, Paul. "Interest Groups in the American Economy." *The Structure of the American Economy, Part I*. Washington, D.C.: National Resource Committee, 1939.
130. Taussig, F.W. and Barker, W.F. "American Corporations and Their Executives." *Quarterly Journal of Economics* 40 (November 1925): 1-51.
131. Theil, Henri. *Principles of Econometrics*. New York: John Wiley & Sons, Inc., 1971.
132. U.S. Congress. Committee on Banking and Currency. *Commercial Banks and Their Trust Activities: Emerging Influence on the American Economy*. Washington, D.C. 1968. A Staff Report.
133. U.S. Temporary National Economic Committee. *The Distribution of Ownership in the 200 Largest Nonfinancial Corporations*. Monograph No. 29. Washington, D.C.: U.S. Government Printing Office, 1940.
134. *The Value Line Investment Survey*. New York: Arnold Bernhard & Co., Inc. Published Weekly.
135. Villajero, Don. "Stock Ownership and the Control of Corporations." *New University Thought* 2 (Winter 1962): 33-77.
136. Ware, Robert F. "A Test of Entrepreneurial vs. Managerial Hypothesis in the Theory of the Firm." Ph.D. dissertation, Michigan State University, 1972.
137. Williamson, John. "Profit, Growth, and Sales Maximization." *Economica* 33 (February 1966): 1-16.

138. Williamson, Oliver E. "A Dynamic Stochastic Theory of Managerial Behavior." In *Prices: Issues in Theory, Practice and Public Policy.* Edited by A. Phillips and O.E. Williamson. Philadelphia, Pennsylvania: University of Pennsylvania Press, 1967.
139. _____. *Corporate Control and Business Behavior: Managerial Objectives in a Theory of the Firm.* Englewood Cliffs, N.J.: Prentice-Hall, 1964.
140. _____. "Corporate Control and the Theory of the Firm." In *Economic Policy and the Regulation of Corporate Securities*, pp. 281-336. Edited by Henry G. Manne. Washington, D.C.: American Enterprise Institute, 1969.
141. Winter, Sidney G., Jr. "Economic 'Natural Selection' and the Theory of the Firm." *Yale Economic Essays* 4 (Spring 1964): 225-72.
142. Wrightsman, Dwayne. "An Analysis of the Extent of the Corporate Ownership and Control by Private Pension Funds." Ph.D. dissertation, Michigan State University, 1964.
143. _____. "Pension Funds and Economic Concentration." *Quarterly Review of Economics and Business* 7 (Winter 1967): 29-36.
144. Wu, Hsiu-Kwang. "Corporate Insider Trading, Profitability and Stock Price Movements." Ph.D. dissertation, University of Pennsylvania, 1963.

Index

Index

Alchian, A., 4, 5, 35, 36, 65-66, 90

Baker, J.C., 23
Baker, S., 26
Barker, W.F., 21, 23
barriers to entry, 46n; for industries in study, 72
Baumol, W.J., 2-4, 7-8, 16-20, 21, 25, 36, 39n, 46n, 50, 52 64, 101, 103
Beard, M., 50
Beazer, W., xii
Berle, Adolf, 1, 3-4, 21, 32, 35-36, 71
Beta coefficient, 105-106
board of directors, composition of, 84, 100
bonus payments, 23-24, 54
Boudreaux, K.J., 42-43, 50-52, 101, 107
Bower, R.S., 52n
Boyle, S.E., 31
Buchanan, J., xii
Buchanan, N.S., 2, 64
Burch, P., 33, 71
bureconic theory of salaries, 9

capital market constraint, 4-5, 34-39
Chandler, A., 104
Chevalier, J., 34
Chin, J.S.Y., 25-26, 40-43, 51n
Ciscel, David H., 26
Cleveland Trust Company, 34
commercial banks, 34
Committee on Banking and Currency, 132
compensation, executive, 16; and control type, 58-84; definition, 69-70, 119-121; size and composition, 23-25
Conference Board, The, 54
control, separation of ownership from, xi, 5; and compensation, 29, 58-84; definitions of, 71-72; and firm age, 95; market for corporate, 35-38; and rate of return, 39-50; and retention policy, 53-54, 93-100; and risk, 50-53, 101-107; summary of effects, 111-114; and tenure policies, 30-31, 85-86; transaction costs of, 37
Cooley, D.E., 40-43, 50, 51n
Cox, E., 94
Crew, M.A., 14-15, 49
Crum, W.L., 94
Cyert, R.M., 3

Dauten, J., 102
De Alessi, L., 31n, 48
deferred compensation, 24, 69, 120

dominant stockholder constraint, 32-35, 55, 61-64
Donaldson, G., 36n
Dooley, P.C., 84
Downs, A., 39n, 46n, 50, 52, 101, 103
Durbrow, B.R., 30

executive: age, 70n, 121n; competition for jobs, 19; income, size and composition, 23-25; promotion incentives, 30-31; tenure, 85-86; turnover, 30-31; utility function, 58-59
externally-controlled firms: defined, 71-72; managerial incentives in, 61-64

Fidelity Management and Research Corporation, 34
Forbes, 72n, 84n
Fortune, 71, 91
free-rider problem, xii, 18
Friedman, M., 4, 35
Furubotn, E., 62

Galbraith, J.K., 3, 10-11, 16-18, 64
Gordon, M., 71
Gordon, R.A., 2, 19, 23-24, 32, 39n, 66, 71, 90, 95, 103-105
Grabowski, H.G., 96, 98-99
growth, firm: maximization of, 8-9; and security, 65n. *See also* size

Hall, M., 47, 49
Hayes, S.L., 37n
heteroscedasticity: in profitability studies, 47; in this study, 74-75
Hicks, J.R., 14
Higgins, R., 2
Hindley, B., 36-37
Hogarty, T.F., 31
Huntsman, B., 26-27, 74

identification problems: in profitability studies, 47-49; in relating income to performance, 27, 92-93
inside information, 28, 48, 92-93
institutional investors, 34-35, 55

Johnston, J., 73n
Jones-Lee, M.W., 14-15, 49
Jorgensen, L.P., 34, 42, 84n
Justice Department, 34

Kamerschen, D., 39-43, 53-54, 94-95

137

Karst, P., 43-44
Kessel, R., 5, 36
Kmenta, J., 73n
Knight, F., 19, 66, 95
Knowles, J.C., 33n
Koch, J.V., 41n
Kolko, G., 33
Kuehn, D.A., 37

Larner, R.J., 28-29, 45-46, 52-53, 58, 101, 107
Leibenstein, H., 3, 14-15
Lewellen, Wilbur, 24-27, 67, 74, 119-121

McGuire, J.W., 25-26
manager-controlled firms: defined, 71-72; managerial incentives in, 64-66
Mann, H.M., 46
Manne, H., 28n, 36, 60
March, J.G., 3
Marris, R., 3, 5, 9-10, 30, 64-65, 95
Marshall, Alfred, 1
Masson, R.T., 27-28, 62
Meade, J.E., 36
Monsen, R.J., 39n, 40-43, 46n, 50, 51n, 52, 101, 103
Moody's Investor Service, 96n
Morgan Guaranty Trust Company, 34
Mueller, D., 49, 95-98
multicollinearity: in compensation studies, 26; in this study, 74-75

Noether, G., 46

organizational slack, 3
owner-managed firms: defined, 71-72; and managerial incentives, 66-67, 117-118

Palmer, J., 33, 44-45, 51-52, 101-102, 103n, 106n, 107
Pechman, J.A., 119
Pejovich, S., 62
Penrose, E., 9
pension plans, 26, 29, 69; computation of, 120
profit, 7; and control type, 39-50; definition of, 70-71; minimum constraint, 13

Radice, H.K., 41n, 45
retained earnings, 11, 16-17; and control type, 53-54, 93-100
risk, 8; and control type, 50-53, 101-107
Roberts, David, 25, 72

Rowley, C.K., 14-15, 49

sales, firm: defined, 71; maximization of, 7-8. *See also* size
sample, 68, 123-124
satisficing, 3, 14
Schumpeter, J.A., 19, 66, 95
Scitovski, T., 2-3
Securities and Exchange Commission, 32, 34, 68
Sheehan, R., 33, 103
Shepherd, W.G., 46
Sherer, F.M., 41n
Sherman, R., xii, 71
Simon, H., 3, 14
Singer Sewing Machine, Inc., 64
Singh, A., 37-38
size, firm: and age, 97; defined, 71; and executive income, 64-65; and security, 11, 12, 16-17
Smith, Adam, 1
Solow, R., 10, 15, 36
Sorenson, R.L., 31, 45-47, 53-54, 94-95, 99
stock options, 64n; computation of, 119-120; as "tax dodge," 11
Sweezy, P., 33

Taussig, F.W., 21, 23
Taussig, R.A., 37n
Temporary National Economic Committee, 32-33
tenure, executive, 84-86
Theil, H., 47n
transaction costs of control, 37, 60

valuation ratio, 37, 75n
Villarejo, D., 34

Wall Street Journal, The, 65
Ware, R., 49
Weiss, L., 47, 49
Williamson, J., 10, 36
Williamson, O.E., 3, 12-20, 30-31, 36, 46n, 53-54, 57, 62, 64, 72, 93-94, 99-100
Winter, S.G., 4, 35
Wrightsman, D., 34n
Wu, H., 28n

X-inefficiency, 14
X-theory, 15-16

About the Author

William A. McEachern was born in 1945 in Portsmouth, New Hampshire. He is now Assistant Professor of Economics at the University of Connecticut, where he has been a member of the faculty since 1973. He graduated *cum laude* in the Honors Program from Holy Cross College in 1967. He received the M.A. in 1969 and the Ph.D. in 1975 from the University of Virginia. From 1969-1971, he served as a U. S. Army officer with the Office of the Secretary of the Army. Dr. McEachern has contributed to the *Virginia Essays in Economics*, and *Economic Inquiry*, plus several edited volumes.